Body Image Deviation in Chronic Schizophrenia

BODY IMAGE DEVIATION IN CHRONIC SCHIZOPHRENIA

REIKO KOIDE AND AKIRA TAMAOKA

Nova Science Publishers, Inc.
New York

For permission to use material from this book please contact us:
Telephone 631-231-7269; Fax 631-231-8175
Web Site: http://www.novapublishers.com

LIBRARY OF CONGRESS CATALOGING-IN-PUBLICATION DATA

Koide, Reiko.
Body image deviation in chronic schizophrenia / Reiko Koide and Akira Tamaoka.
p. ; cm.
Includes bibliographical references and index.
ISBN 978-1-60456-655-0 (softcover)
1. Schizophrenia. 2. Body image disturbance. I. Tamaoka, Akira. II. Title.
[DNLM: 1. Schizophrenia--complications. 2. Body Image. 3. Perceptual Distortion. WM 203 K79b 2008]
RC514.K64 2008
616.89'8--dc22

2008013840

Published by Nova Science Publishers, Inc. ✣ New York

CONTENTS

PREFACE

BACKGROUND

Body image aberration in schizophrenia was earlier conceived as delusional and hallucinatory symptoms. However, perceptions of schizophrenia have changed dramatically, especially with the concept of negative symptoms in the 1980s and in the 1990s, to include the neurocognitive aspects of schizophrenia. Deviations in schizophrenics' body image from the standard underlying various behaviors or allegations concerning the body should be now refocused. In this chapter, using the Body Image Questionnaire (BIQ), comprised of three hypothetical components, anatomical, functional and psychological, attempts were made to resolve some primary questions. They were (1) whether or not there is any related clinical characteristics to schizophrenic body image abberation, (2) whether there are aberrant components of body image specific to schizophrenia, (3) whether or not there is unique link between depression and body image in schizophrenia.

METHODS

In study 1, correlations between body image assessed by the BIQ and clinical characteristics as positive and negative symptoms assessed by SAPS and SANS, insight assessed by SAI, and daily dose of conventional antipsychotic drugs were examined. In study 2, three components of body image, that is, anatomical, functional and psychological, were compared between schizophrenic and non-schizophrenic groups. In study 3, the correlation between depression assessed by SDS and body image assessed by the BIQ was examined. In these studies, 93 chronic schizophrenics, 177 normal adults, and 43 patients with anxiety disorders according to DSM-IV criteria, were examined. In studies 4-5, the additional finding of Rorschach percepts concerning body image in schizophrenia was reported.

Results

Schizophrenics' body image aberration proved to be independent of symptoms and medication. It was also shown that the aberration proved to be limited to functional imageries, and that the anatomical component remained intact. As to depression, a specific link of body image, especially with functional imageries, with the depression characteristic to schizophrenia was found.

Conclusion

All these results showed that body image aberration in schizophrenics is not the result of symptoms or effects of conventional neuroleptic medications, but they are germane to schizophrenia, which is comprised of aberration mainly in functional body imageries. This body image deviation proved to be linked to some serious depressive signs and symptoms in schizophrenia. The subsidiary findings, that is, the Rorschach percepts as a mass of flesh quite often seen in schizophrenia, are congruent with the main findings that schizophrenic patients showed an anticipation of becoming unmovable.

Keywords: body image, schizophrenia, symptom, insight, depression, perception

Chapter 1

INTRODUCTION

SCHIZOPHRENICS' BODY IMAGE ABERRATION: AN OVERVIEW

Since the time of Kraepelin (1919) and Bleuler (1911/1950), schizophrenics' deviant perceptions, feelings, and beliefs concerning their bodies have been described. In this chapter, the symptoms relevant to body image aberration that have been discussed for over the past half century, as well as psychological measures that were developed to understand these aberrations, are reviewed, to lead to the current status and future prospects for the study of the body image aberration in schizophrenia.

(1) Symptoms Relevant To Body Image Aberration

Disturbances of body experience in schizophrenic patients occur frequently. They have been observed as somatic delusions (McGlichrist and Cutting, 1995), coenaesthesis (Huber, 1957/1971; Rohricht and Priebe, 1997, Schmoll and Koch, 1989; Schmoll, 1994), disturbances of pain perception (Dworkin and Caligor, 1988; Rosenthal et al., 1990; Dworkin, 1994; Guieu et al., 1994; Lautenbacher and Krieg, 1994), out-of-body experiences (Blackmore, 1986; Twemlow et al., 1982), dysmorphophobia (Connolly and Gipson, 1978; Hay, 1983; Birtchnell, 1988; Snaith, 1992; Philips and McEloroy, 1993; deLeon et al., 1989; Phillips et al., 1994), and self-injury or self mutilation (Feldman, 1988; Burgess, 1991; Martin and Gattaz, 1991; Sonneburn and Vanstraelen, 1992 ; Weiser et al., 1993; Kennedy and Feldmann, 1994). In addition, the effects of body-oriented psychotherapy have been suggested (Darby, 1968; Berman, 1972).

According to Roehricht and Priebe (1997) in a report by Huber and Zerbin-Rueden (1979), although symptoms relevant to body distortion were seen in more than 74% of cases of schizophrenia, little attention has been paid to the evaluation of such symptoms. These symptoms are not included as a prominent component in psychometric approaches to measuring symptoms, such as the Brief Psychiatric Rating Scale, BPRS, (Overall and Gorham, 1962) or the Positive and Negative Symptoms Scale, PANSS (Kay et al., 1987). It is, however, not fair to regard that the issue as being rather neglected. Specifically, bizarre somatopsychic phenomena, e.g., feelings that the body is "being radiated," "being controlled by others," and "being cut up" have been reported in schizophrenia. Some of these abnormal body perceptions have been designated as "Schneiderian first rank symptoms" (Schneider, 1959/1976). Dysmorphophobia was relabeled as "one of the Somatoform Disorders" in 1980. "Body Dysmorphic Disorder," and its counterpart, "Delusional Disorder, Somatic Subtype" in 1987, were included in the *Diagnostic and Statistical Manual of Mental Disorders* (American Psychiatric Association, 1987), which produced considerable concern over delusions regarding appearance of the body (deLeon et al., 1989; Phillips et al., 1994). First, studies of these symptoms relevant to disturbances in body experiences in schizophrenia are reviewed to give an overview of how the problems have been described and treated.

Before Antipsychotics

Even in the era before antipsychotic agents, body image was rather attractive to those who studied the psychopathology of schizophrenia. Since Wernicke foreshadowed the idea of body image in his concept of "somatopsyche," this whole psychological field has been recognized as important in the understanding of psychotic patients, especially in relation to hallucinatory and delusional disturbances (Schilder, 1935; Angyal, 1936; Gerstmann, 1942; Bychowsky,1943).

The initial study of body image was a description of phantom limb. It was succeeded by neurological research from the 1910s to the 1950s (Head, 1911/1926; Pick, 1922; Schilder, 1935), and body image was conceived as the equivalent of "body schema" or "postural schema." This became the traditional definition of the concept. It was introduced to the field of psychiatry by Schilder (1935), and attempts were made to find similar distortions in psychiatric patients (Schilder, 1935; Angyal, 1936).

Bodily Hallucination and Somatic Delusion

Lukianowicz (1967) and McGlichrist and Cutting (1995) classified somatic delusions of psychotic cases including schizophrenia, showing that bodily delusions and hallucinations occur mostly inseparably. Bodily hallucination and somatic delusion have been treated as coenaesthesis in non-English speaking psychiatry, especially in Germany, where it was often reported to herald the onset of schizophrenia (Huber 1957,1971; Rohricht and Priebe, 1997; Schmoll and Koch, 1989; Schmoll, 1994).

Disturbances of Pain Perception

A disorder of proprioception in schizophrenic patients was earlier described by Rado (1959) as a basic element in schizophrenia. He speculated that extensive proprioceptive deficits could lead to distorted awareness of body image and eventually to the thought disorder characteristic of schizophrenia. Rosenbaum et al. (1965) and Ritzler and Rosenbaum (1974) conducted a series of experiments based on his theory with schizophrenic and non-schizophrenic subjects using weight discrimination as a measure of proprioception. They found that schizophrenics performed almost as well as normals do when asked to discriminate heavy weights, but did not discriminate light weights nearly as well as normals. Since light weights do not provide as much proprioceptive feedback as do heavy weights, these results were interpreted as demonstrating a proprioceptive deficit in the schizophrenics. These results, however, were not replicated by other authors (Ritzler, 1977; Leventhal et al., 1982), who showed that a proprioceptive deficit is not unique to schizophrenia.

Since the time of Kraepelin and Bleuler, "pain insensitivity" or "reduced sensitivity to pain" in schizophrenia has been documented. Kraepelin (1919) observed that patients with schizophrenia are often "less sensitive to bodily discomfort; they endure uncomfortable positions, pricks of a needle, injuries…burn themselves with their cigar, hurt themselves." Bleuler (1911/1950) noted that even in well-oriented patients one may often observe the presence of a complete analgesia which includes the deeper parts of the body as well as the skin. The patients "pluck out an eye, sit down on a hot stove and receive severe burns".

Although some authors reported that schizophrenic patients suffer headache (Varsamis and Adamson, 1976; Watson et al., 1981; Philips and Hunter, 1982; Torrey, 1989), the prevalence of pain complaints in schizophrenia appears to be lower than in other psychiatric disorders (Merskey, 1965; Spear, 1967; Delapaine et al., 1978; Watson et al., 1981). There are many descriptions of pain insensitivity in schizophrenia by surgeons and internists (Arieti, 1945; Marchand,

1959; West and Hecker, 1952; Vanderkampt, 1970; Apter, 1981, Fishbain 1982; Bickerstaff et al., 1988, Katz et al., 1990; Rosenthal et al., 1990). Dworkin (1994) reviewed the literature on this issue and argued that the insensitivity, although currently neglected, has important implications for physical health, self-mutilation, homelessness, premorbid development, and affective flattening in schizophrenic patients. Lautenbacher and Krieg (1994) also reviewed the literature and pointed out that pain insensitivity is important in elucidating pathophysiological mechanisms because pain perception is controlled by neurochemical and neurohormonal functions known to be affected by psychiatric disease processes. Guieu et al. (1994), however, assessed the pain thresholds of ten schizophrenic patients and ten controls by measuring the leg flexion nociceptive reflex threshold, and concluded that in most cases the increase in pain threshold is the result of attitude and not alterations in brain function.

Out-of-Body Experiences

A number of studies have pointed out the confusion in the existing psychiatric literature concerning the status of consciousness in which there is an altered perception of the mind/body relationship. They defined out-of-body experience (OBE) as an altered state of consciousness in which one's mind or awareness is experienced as separated from one's physical body. They argued that the increasing numbers of patients who are involved in such phenomena, traditionally classified as psychopathological, should not be treated in the way that a symptom is usually treated (e.g., interpretation or medication) but should be viewed by a physician with "benign neglect" (Twemlow, et al., 1982).

Gabbard et al. developed a questionnaire, Profile of Out-of-Body Experiences, POBE, that included 51 items based on reports of near-death experiences, mystical-religious literature, and philosophical-occult-psychotic literature describing OBE experiences. They tried to clarify this group of phenomena by differentiating OBE from depersonalization, autoscopic phenomena, and schizophrenic body distortions (such as boundary loss). They selected seven points to differentiate OBE from the disturbances in corporal perception found in schizophrenia. That is, the bodily distortions in schizophrenic patients are characterized by loss of reality testing, chronic difficulty with delineation of body boundaries, varied bodily distortions, being uncertain of the location of the body, profound regression in personality, blurred identity, and being experienced as "going crazy," whereas those experiencing OBE show intact reality testing, have episodic and short-lived experiences, basically unvaried distortion, are certain of their location, show no evidence of regression, have an intact identity, and are not experienced as "going crazy."

Blackmore (1986) administered POBE to schizophrenic patients, along with two other questionnaires to assess perception and symptoms, and showed that there is no evidence to consider the typical OBE as pathological or as symptomatic of schizophrenia.

Dysmorphophobia

Extreme concern with aspects of personal appearance was called dysmorphophobia by Morselli in 1886 (Birtchnell, 1988; Phillips, 1991), who defined it as "a subjective feeling of ugliness or physical defect that the patient feels is noticeable to others, although his appearance is within normal limits." Despite its relative neglect in American psychiatry, it is now termed "Somatoform Disorder" in DSM III (1980), "Body Dysmorphic Disorder (BDD)" in DSM III-R with its counterpart, "Delusional Disorder, Somatic Subtype (DDSS)" (1987). It is a distressing and impairing disorder that may lead to occupational and social dysfunction as well as unnecessary and costly cosmetic surgery and dermatologic treatment (Phillips, 1991), and an increase in this disorder has been reported (Phillips et al., 1993; Hollander et al., 1993). It is still described with the term BDD under the heading of Somatoform Disorder in DSM-IV (1994).

In the 19th century, the term "dysmorphophobia" described those patients who present with "a fear of being misshapen" when in fact objectively they have no cause for complaint. However, numerous reports of dysmorphophobia in psychiatric morbidity, including schizophrenia, have been reported (Connolly and Gipson, 1978; Edgerton et al., 1960; Jacobsen et al., 1960; Hay, 1970). In the 1980s, there were continuing debates as to its status as a symptom or discrete psychiatric illness; that is, it is not a phobia because there is no fear of physical abnormality per se—the ugliness of others is tolerated. It was remarked that dysmorphophobia is non-specific as a symptom and can occur in a variety of different psychiatric syndromes, from a sensitive personality development to an attenuated schizophrenic illness (Hay, 1970/1983).

In the 1940s to the 1960s, psychodynamic theories attempted to recognize that a complaint about appearance might be understood in terms of psychological defense mechanisms (Meyer et al., 1960; Jacobsen et al., 1960; Linn and Goldman, 1949; Hill and Silver, 1950). Body parts took on a psychological significance and symbolic function, and a complaint might reflect an underlying conflict. However, reports of excellent results from surgery on the minimally deformed led to criticism to these theories, suggesting neurotic, and even psychotic, patients can benefit from cosmetic surgery (Edgerton et al., 1960; Hay, 1973).

Although the original definition of dysmorphophobia states that the appearance is within normal limits, diagnostic criteria proposed for dysmorphophobia allow for a slight physical anomaly to be present, but with the patient's concern judged disproportionately great (Andreasen and Bardach, 1977). Birtchnell (1988) regarded it as important to maintain a distinction between those patients with minimal deformity (the normal but less than attractive) who might considerably benefit from surgery and those with primary dysmorphophobia distinguished by the vagueness of the complaint, e.g., "the skin under my eyes joins my nose in a funny way," where surgery is contraindicated, rather than, for example, "the tip of my nose is rather bulbous."

The disorder once termed dysmorphophobia was renamed body dysmorphic disorder (BDD) in DSM III-R. As Snaith (1992) reviewed, DSM III-R considered the disorder under two headings: (1) delusional disorder, somatic type, and (2) body dysmorphic disorder. The distinctions between these two categories rests on whether the bodily concern has the characteristics of a true delusion, but a clear distinction cannot always be made. DSM III-R differentiated BDD, a nonpsychotic somatoform disorder in which insight is present, from its delusional counterpart, a psychotic disorder in which insight is absent. The delusional variant of BDD was reported as a more severe form of the disorder (Phillips et al., 1994).

Self-Injury or Self Mutilation

Self-injurious behaviour of various sorts occurs in an appreciable number of individuals with schizophrenia, as well as in those with other disorders (Burgess, 1991). Self-mutilation has been defined as "painful , destructive and injurious acts upon the body without the apparent intent to commit suicide" (Pattison and Kahan, 1983). Reports of self-mutilation in patients with schizophrenia include descriptions of unilateral and bilateral eye enucleation (Feldman, 1988; Kennedy and Feldmann, 1994), self-laceration (Shore et al., 1978; Sweeny and Zamecnik, 1981), and self-amputation of various parts of the body, including the hand (Schweitzer, 1990), breast (Coons et al., 1986), ear (Silva, et al., 1989; Weiser et al., 1993), penis and testicles (Schweitzer, 1990; Martin and Gattaz, 1991), and in what is arguably the most extreme case reported to date, virtually the entire face (Scheftel et al., 1986).

Burgess (1991) studied the relationship of depression and cognitive impairment to self-injury in psychiatric patients including schizophrenics, showing that self-injury was correlated with neurocognitive deficits in borderline and schizophrenic groups.

Body-Oriented Psychotherapy

An early theoretical assumption, currently recognized as invalid, was that the core disturbance in schizophrenia is a breakdown of ego boundaries leading to a dedifferentiation of the self from the non-self (Federn, 1952; Freeman et al., 1958). According to this theory, what is sensed as thought (a process occurring within the mental and physical boundary) is no longer distinguished from what is sensed as lying outside the ego boundary (Berman, 1972). Psychoanalytic theorists have stressed the important role the individual's body plays in bringing about the formation of the ego (e.g., Federn, 1952; Fenichel, 1954; Ferenczi, 1926; Freud, 1962), and the maintenance of the distinction between ego and non-ego was a controversial issue for psychotherapeutic treatment of schizophrenia.

Des Lauriers (1962) theorized that the recovery process in schizophrenia could be conceptualized as a progressive definition and demarcation of the schizophrenic's ego boundaries through a systematically increased awareness of body limits and bodily self. In order to accomplish this, the psychotherapist attempted to stimulate in the schizophrenic patient awareness of, and interest in, the bodily self as the separating boundary from that which is not himself (Darby, 1968; Des Lauriers, 1962). Studies conducted with an inkblot boundary index developed by Fisher and Cleveland (1958), the Barrier and Penetration scores, lend some support to the above conception of schizophrenia and the recovery process, in that schizophrenics were differentiated from neurotics and normals on the basis of their lower Barrier and higher Penetration scores (Fisher and Cleveland, 1958; Reitman and Cleveland, 1964; Holtzman et al., 1961) and that as a schizophrenic improved clinically, his Penetration scores decreased (Cleveland, 1960a). Fisher and Cleveland (1968) suggested that special treatment efforts, aimed at re-identifying and redefining bodily limits, should improve these patients. Because a question arises as to whether directly focusing the schizophrenic patient's awareness and attention on his own body can effect a redefinition of boundaries, attempts were made to demonstrate that focusing on somatic stimuli leads to subsequent changes in inkblot boundary indexes, implying, at least, that it can (Fisher and Renik, 1966; Renik and Fisher, 1968). Attempts were also made to expect alteration of body image change in these indexes by inducing somatic awareness in groups of hospitalized schizophrenics (Darby, 1968). Quinlan and Harrow (1974) examined the boundary in a sample of acute schizophrenics by the use of four types of Rorschach indexes including Barrier and Penetration scores. Their results support the hypothesis that schizophrenics give certain types of responses considered indicative of boundary disturbance, such as contamination responses, although Barrier and Penetration indexes are more benign signs of boundary diffusion.

(2) Psychological Measurement of Body Image Aberration

The above observations have led to an assumption that body image aberration or deviation exists in schizophrenia, and that it is related to the core of schizophrenia. Attempts were made, using the Rorschach test (Quinlan and Harrow 1974; Fisher and Cleveland, 1958/1968; Fisher, 1963), Drawing test (Kokonis, 1972) and inquiries (Fisher and Seidner, 1963; Chapman et al., 1978; Coleman et al., 1996; Koide, 1985; Oosthuizen et al., 1998), to point to characteristic deviations of body image in schizophrenic patients. These are the Body Distortion Questionnaire, BDQ, (Rohricht and Priebe, 1996), the Perceptual Aberration Scale, PAS, (Coleman et al., 1996; Chapman et al., 1978), Dysmorphic Concern Questionnaire, DCQ (Oosthuizen et al., 1998), and the present Body Image Questionnaire, BIQ (Koide, 1985). However, none of these measures are regarded as well-established (Rohricht and Prieb, 1997).

Projective Method

Early attempts to measeure body image aberrations were made through indirect means, that is, projective techniques. Figure-drawing techniques (Goodenough, 1928; Machover, 1949), have been used often by researchers (Cancro, 1971; Jasker and Reed, 1963; Sugarman and Cancro, 1964); however, most of the differences between schizophrenic and normal subjects appear to reflect nothing more than general inadequacy of drawing skill by schizophrenics (Swensen, 1957/1968). Barrier and penetration percepts on the Rorschach Test were inferred from body image (Fisher and Cleveland, 1958/1968). Barrier percepts are ones that emphasize peripheral-boundary-defining qualities of the percepts (e.g., flower pot or knife in armor). Penetration percepts involve penetration of outer surfaces of things (e.g., squashed bug or x-ray picture). Lowered barrier scores and heightened penetration scores have been reported in schizophrenia (Fisher and Cleveland, 1958/1968; Reitman and Cleveland, 1964; Holtzman et al., 1961/64). A lack of difference has also been reported (Jasker and Reed, 1963). While support for schizophrenic deviancy on the barrier and penetration scores is strong, acceptance of such evidence as support for schizophrenic body-image aberration requires belief in the projective hypothesis (Chapman et al., 1978).

Experimental Measurement

More direct attempts were made to measure body image aberration in the laboratory setting. Traub et al. (1967) performed an experiment in which the subjects adjust a body-distorting mirror until they believe that it reflects them accurately, with the result that schizophrenic patients erred more than the normal control subjects. Controversial results were presented in studies in which the patients were asked to judge the size of their own body. Cleveland (1960) and Cleveland et al. (1962) reported that schizophrenics overestimate the size of their various body parts (hand, foot, stomach, heart) more than control subjects do, although Weckowicz and Sommer (1960) found that schizophrenics underestimate sizes of their hands and feet. Dillon (1962) and Fisher (1966) found no difference between schizophrenic and normal subjects.

Questionnaire Measurement

The first questionnaire that attempted to measure body image aberration in schizophrenia is the Body Experience Questionnaire, BEQ, which is a true-false questionnaire developed by Fisher and Seidner (1963) and Fisher (1964). Their findings showed greater body image aberration in schizophrenics than in non-schizophrenic subjects, but their BEQ focused to a large extent on hypochondriacal concerns and feelings of body inadequacy rather than the more extreme psychosis-like deviancy of perception of the body that is usually attributed to schizophrenia.

Chapman et al. (1978) developed another questionnaire to measure schizophrenic body image aberration, the Perceptual Aberration Scale, PAS, which is composed of 28 items and a four-point rating sale. Items were intended to tap five kinds of deviant experiences that are uncommon in normal people. The experiences dealt with (a) unclear boundaries of the body, (b) feeling of unreality of, or estrangement from, parts of the body, (c) a sense of deterioration of the body, (d) perceptions of change in size, relative proportions, or spatial relationships of body parts, and (e) changes in the appearance of the body. The scale was standardized on normal control groups. Male schizophrenics reported more body image aberration than normal control subjects, but only a portion of the schizophrenics were deviant. In addition, schizophrenic body image aberrations were negatively correlated with time since first hospitalization and had no correlation with the Physical Anhedonia Scale (Chapman et al., 1976) for schizophrenia, suggesting that the two scales, PAS and Physical Anhedonia Scale, may identify alternative manifestations of proneness toward the same schizophrenia, that is, schizophrenia and schizophrenia-proneness. Coleman et al. (1996) administered PAS to a sample of 2000 students to detect a group of schizotypy in a study conducted to examine the empirical links between schizophrenia and schizotypic psychopathology. Through comparisons of thought disorder assessed by the Thought Disorder Index, TDI (Coleman et al., 1993), between high and low PAS groups, the authors supported the hypothesis that psychometrically identified schizotypic individuals tapped by PAS display thought disorder similar to that of schizophrenia.

Oosthuizen et al. (1998) developed a four-point questionnaire, the Dysmorphic Concern Questionnaire, DCQ, to assess dysmorphic concerns, and tried to establish a correlation with clinical variables. The DCQ was loosely based on the General Health Questionnaire, GHQ. A series of seven statements was devised, based on the dysmorphic concern literature, to capture the essence of the problem (e.g., concern about physical appearance, considering oneself misshapen) and past attempts to deal with the problem (e.g., consulting a plastic surgeon, covering up supposed defects). The DCQ was administered to 63 patients including 33 schizophrenics. The results showed dysmorphic concern is often a reflection of cognitive set rather than a diagnosis itself.

The Body Image Questionnaire, BIQ, is a seven-step self-rating questionnaire with 59 body referring items, especially devised to measure schizophrenic body image deviation (Koide, 1985). The BIQ was developed on the basis of the clinical observations made through contact with chronic schizophrenic patients by clinicians and the attempts to grasp their deviations through assessing rather persistent attitudes or feelings toward the patients' own bodies, which are measurable on a graded continuum with those of normals. Thus, what is assessed by the BIQ is not a psychosis-like body distortion experience itself but an underlying readiness for observable aberrant behaviors including distorted body experiences. The patients' deviated concern about their body is revealed by observations. A middle-aged female schizophrenic patient tried to eat her glasses to exemplify the strength of her teeth (image of strong teeth). A young male patient continued to reject walking outside the hospital in the treatment programs because he felt tight like a stone when he tried to go out (image of tightness caused by relaxation). One young female patient talked about her wish to commit suicide because, she said, she wanted to avoid situations in which she imagined herself unable to move her own body by herself (image of becoming immobile). The items of the BIQ were arranged to include three prospectively hypothetical components: namely, anatomical, functional and other psychological elements such as mood and primitive sensation.

Objective of the Study

A wide variety of studies has appeared on body image aberration in schizophrenia; however, the problem inherent in schizophrenic body image aberration remains elusive. Earlier, the body image problems in schizophrenia were regarded as something related to psychotic symptoms, particularly with delusion and hallucination. Our perceptions of the schizophrenia have changed dramatically, particularly over the past two decades. During 1980s, the predominant view of the phenomenology of schizophrenia broadened beyond a narrow focus on psychotic symptoms to include negative symptoms, proprioceptive deficits, and self-injury representing body image problems. In the 1990s, another fundamental change in our perception of the disorder occurred. With this change, we have expanded the phenomenology of schizophrenia even further, beyond symptoms altogether, to include a strong emphasis on neurocognitive aspects of schizophrenia (Green and Neuchterlein, 1999).

Schizophrenia has consequently been investigated using "neuropsychological" procedures in order to uncover evidence of discrete neurological damage or dysfunction that may account for the great impairments in judgment, attention, concentration, planning ability and anticipation. In the late 1970s, a new era of neuropsychological study of schizophrenia began with three different review articles in which the low performance on neuropsychological test in functional patients was compared to organic patients (Goldstein, 1978; Heaton et al., 1978; Malec, 1978), and with the initial publication of in vivo evidence of ventricular enlargement in schizophrenia, as revealed by computerized tomography (CT) (Johonstone et al., 1976; Weinberger et al., 1979).

Focus has been on clarifying the relationships between neurocognitive deficits and psychotic symptoms (Cornblatt et al., 1985; Green and Walker, 1985; Neuchterlein et al., 1986; Green et al., 1992) and negative symptoms (Neuchterlein et al., 1986; Censits et al., 1997; Buchanan et al., 1997), between neurocognitive deficits and functional outcome (Green, 1996), between neurocognitive deficits and insight (Silverstein and Zerwic, 1985; Young et al., 1993; Lysaker and Bell, 1994; Cuesta and Peralta, 1994) and social cognition (Schneider et al., 1995; Bryson et al., 1997). In a current overview, Green and Nuechterlein (1999) searched for meaningful psychopharmacological and cognitive/behavioral interventions for neurocognitive deficits in schiziophrenia. Conventional antipsychotic agents are generally effective for psychotic symptoms, but their effects on neurocognition are relatively weak (Cassens et al., 1990; Strauss, 1993). Novel antipsychotic medications are more encouraging (Hagger et al., 1993; Green et al., 1997; Jeste et al., 1998; Keefe et al., 1999; Kern et al., 1999; Meltzer and McGurk, 1999). Conventional antipsychotic medications involve much coadministration of anticholinergic medications (e.g., benoztropine mesylate) that are known to have a negative effect on neurocognition (Spohn and Strauss, 1989).

To consider body image aberration in the above context, which deficit of body image comes from symptoms and which from medication should be clarified first. The questions are (1) Is body image aberration a result of symptoms seen in attenuated schizophrenic illness? (2) Is body image aberration an effect of medications? (3) What is the schizophrenics' body image's inherently aberrational part? Is there any intact part? (4) Is it remediable by behavioral/cognitive or psychopharmacological intervention? A full investigation of these basic questions is now required. Each section in this chapter is the attempt to clarify these basic problems.

Chapter 2

STUDIES USING BODY IMAGE QUESTIONNAIRE (BIQ)

STUDY 1. BODY IMAGE ABERRATION AND CLINICAL CHARACTERISTICS

Introduction

In the era of pre-antipsychotics, disturbance of body experiences in schizophrenia had been documented as pathological experiences, especially in relation to hallucinatory and delusional disturbances. Since the 1970s, several concepts about the course of schizophrenia and recovery from it have been developed in the search for new perspectives (Strauss 1989; Harding et al., 1992). Because there is a growing interest in the recovery phase of schizophrenia, their body image characteristics should be refocused as multi-phased deviation from the normal experiences. In this context, the body image should be redefined rather comprehensively as persistent attitudes and feelings toward one's own body, which would preserve deleterious as well as ameliorative effects in the illness-environment interaction of disorder and recovery. In addition, with the availability of neuroleptics since mid. 1950s, undesirable physical reactions caused by drugs may also contribute to negative body image.

The aim of the study in this section was to reexamine the body image distortion perceived by schizophrenics, using the Body Image Questionnaire, BIQ, (Koide,1982/1985). Special inquiries were made concerning the influence of the clinical variables such as positive and negative symptoms, insight and neuroleptic dosage on body image aberration. The questions addressed in this sections are (1) What are the components of body images? (2) Which phases of body image are aberrant in schizophrenia? (3) Which aberrant body images are related to symptoms? (4) Which aberrant body images are associated with favorable signs of remission? (5) Is body image aberration related to neuroleptic dosage?

Method

Assessment of Body Image Deviation

Body image was assessed using the BIQ, a seven-step self-rating scale (scored as 1 to 7) with three hypothetical components, anatomical, functional and psychological. (See Appendix 1.)

Assessment of Clinical Characteristics

Positive symptoms were assessed using the Scale for Assessment of Positive Symptoms, SAPS, (Andreasen, 1983). Negative symptoms were assessed using the Scale for Assessment of Negative Symptoms, SANS, (Andreasen, 1981). Insight was assessed through Schedule for Assessing Insight, SAI, which comprises three main component scores that include acceptance, recognition of illness, and relabeling of pathological experiences, and one supplemental component, i.e., the hypothetical contradiction, which measures amenability to delusional experiences (David, 1990).

Subjects

The study sample consisted of 93 chronic schizophrenics; 44 were men and 49 were women. The mean (SD) age of the patients was 48.5 (10.1) years. All of them were inpatients at chronic psychiatric wards of a mental hospital in Ibaraki Prefecture in Japan. They were diagnosed as schizophrenic, on the basis of medical records, according to DSM-IV criteria (Subtypes: 24 Paranoid types, 40 Disorganized types, 25 Residual types, 4 Undifferentiated types). The mean (SD) duration of hospitalization was 24.1 (10.6) years, and the mean (SD) age of onset was 24.0 (7.0) years old. Their mean (SD) dose of neuroleptics was 469.8 (397.5) mg/day of chlorpromazine equivalent dose. The mean SAPS scores of the subjects was 26.2. The mean of SANS scores was 67.8. The mean SAI score was 8.4. The normal control group was comprised of 177 normally functioning adults of whom 78 were men and 99 were women. The mean (SD) age was 44.9 (12.6) years old. The normal adults were attending university summer school classes in psychology, and were confirmed to be normal by the General Health Questionnaire, the GHQ (short form, Goldberg, 1972; Goldberg and Williams, 1988). All subjects were informed of the purpose of the study and actively participated with written informed consent. (See Table 1.)

Table 1. Demographic and clinical characteristics of subjects. (Studies 1 and 5.)

	Schizophrenic (N=93)	Normal (N=177)
Demographic characteristics		
Mean Age	48.5	44.9
Gender (% male)	47.3	44.1
Clinical characteristics	Mean (Range)	
Age of Onset	24.0 (14-45)	
Years of Hospitalization	24.1 (3-47)	
Dose of CPZ (mg/day)	469.8 (30-2156)	
SAPS	26.2 (0-94)	
SANS	67.8 (9-152)	
SDS	42.5 (24-64)	
SAI (Insight)	8.4 (0-14)	

Data Analysis

Comparisons of Means of each BIQ Item Scores

The means of the scores of 59 BIQ items were compared between schizophrenic and normal control groups using t-test.

Factor Analysis of the Body Image Questionnaire

On the bases of tentative preliminary analysis, 32 out of the original 59 items that proved to be not relevant to the factor analysis were excluded. However, two exceptional functional items (items 37, 41) from the excluded non-contributing items that proved to be important for discrimination when each item score was compared were re-included. The items of the final version pertain to smallness (items 8, 40, 54, 55), fatness (items 15, 28, 56) and roundness (items 24, 52) for the anatomical body image component; difficulty in manipulating his/her own body into action (items 9, 13, 21), lack of strength (items 1, 3), unusual concern over digestive functions (items 38, 53) and exceptional criterion-oriented standards (items 37, 41) for the functional component; and dissatisfaction and ugliness (items 10, 12, 27, 32), lack of vitality (items 31, 59) and fragility (items 19, 26, 39) for the psychological component.

The combined (schizophrenic and normal) data of the three BIQ hypothetical components, viz., anatomical, functional and psychological, were separately factor-analyzed using varimax rotation as the principal method, and the means of the factor scores were compared between the schizophrenic and normal control groups using *t*-tests. The factors that proved to be significant in differentiating schizophrenic and normal groups were compared further between the schizophrenic subgroups using *t*-tests. The schizophrenic subgroups were compared according to high (above or equal to mean) and low (lower than mean) scores on subscales and total scores of SAPS, SANS and SAI. Sub-grouping was also done according to the clinical factors of years of hospitalization and age at onset of disease, as well as daily equivalent dose of chlorpromazine. The SPSS (version 10) was used for statistical analysis.

Results

Group Differences of the BIQ Item Scores

The 23 out of 59 BIQ items proved to be differentiating two diagnostic groups. They were being weak, being prone to sickness, being underdeveloped, being dirty, moving slowly, being poor at athletics, being prone to losing balance, being prone to injury, being numb, being clumsy with hands, being prone to catching colds, speaking with a feeble voice, being always gloomy, being unable to work in dark rooms, being susceptible to infection, being unable to move his/her body freely, having a weak heart, minding being touched by others, being meager, not being prone to becoming excited, having weak teeth, having unusually long arms and being listless. (See Table 2.)

Table 2. Means of BIQ items differentiating diagnostic groups. (Study 1.)

	Schizophrenic	Normal
01. My body is weak.	3.913	3.175***
03. I often get sick.	3.774	2.943***
06. My body is underdeveloped.	3.612	3.176**
07. My body is clean. ®	3.065	2.604**
09. I move slowly	4.193	3.649**
13. I am good at athletics.®	4.301	3.556**
17. I often lose my balance.	3.591	3.153*
19. I am often injured.	4.010	3.508**

	Schizophrenic	Normal
23. My mood is numb.	4.279	3.875*
25. I am clumsy with my hands.	4.064	3.593*
26. I seldom catch a cold. ®	4.173	3.519**
29. My voice is feeble.	4.011	3.491**
31. I am always cheerful. ®	3.752	3.255**
37. I can work well in dark rooms. ®	5.258	4.429***
39. My body is susceptible to infection.	3.892	3.278**
41. I cannot move my body freely.	3.239	2.858*
42. My heart is strong. ®	3.397	2.949*
43. I don't mind being touched by others. ®	4.591	4.000**
44. My body is not meager. ®.	3.709	3.339*
45. I seldom get excited.	4.043	3.653*
47. My teeth are weak.	4.826	4.079***
55. My arms are unusually long. ®	3.989	3.680*
59. I always feel energetic.®	3.957	3.491**

*P<0.05, **P<0.01, ***P<0.001.

Factor Analysis and Obtained Differential Factors

Factor Analyses

Factor analyses of the three BIQ components, anatomical, functional, and psychological, using varimax rotation as the principal method, identified three factors with eigenvalues greater than 1 for each component. All items except two (items 37 and 41) had substantial loading on each of the factors. Total variances explained were 47.15%, 52.16% and 44.96%, respectively. Each of the three anatomical factors was composed of items indicating the images of smallness, fatness and roundness, respectively. Each of the three functional factors was composed of items indicating the images of dullness in movement, powerlessness and unusually strong gastrointestinal function, respectively. Each of the three psychological factors was composed of items indicating the images of dissatisfaction, lifelessness and fragility, respectively. (See Table 3 and 4.)

Table 3. Factor structure of BIQ. (Study 1.)

Items of BIQ components	Factors and Factor Loadings			h^2
Anatomical	*A-1*	*A-2*	*A-3*	
55. My arms are short.	0.716			0.539
08. I am short.	0.65			0.463
54. My legs are short.	0.636			0.418
40. My hands are small.	0.457			0.239
28. I am fat.		0.796		0.673
15. My body is not skinny.		0.792		0.629
56. My neck is short.		0.437		0.348
24. My body is not rough.			0.731	0.536
52. My body is round.			0.413	0.401
Functional	*F-1*	*F-2*	*F-3*	
13. I am poor at athletics.	0.808			0.654
09. I move slowly	0.783			0.644
21. I walk slowly.	0.693			0.492
37. I cannot work well in dark rooms.				0.027
03. I often get sick.		0.881		0.804
01. My body is weak.		0.802		0.693
41. I cannot move my body freely.				0.250
38. My stomach is unusually strong.			0.812	0.666
53. My bowels are unusually strong.			0.673	0.462
Psychological	*P-1*	*P-2*	*P-3*	
32. My body is unattractive.	0.693			0.535
27. I am satisfied with my body.	0.684			0.487
12. My body is ugly.	0.671			0.476
10. My body is defective.	0.568			0.385
59. I always feel listless.		0.933		0.903
31. I am always gloomy.		0.506		0.290
26. I often catch colds.			0.586	0.352
39. My body is susceptible to infection.			0.554	0.339
19. I am often injured.			0.496	0.279

Note: Only items that loaded at >.400 are shown.

Table 4. Means of factor scores in schizophrenic and control groups. (Study 1.)

Anatomical Factors	Schizophrenic	Control
A-1. Smallness	0.092	-0.047
A-2. Fatness	0.114	-0.058
A-3. Roundness	0.057	0.029
Functional Factors		
F-1. Dullness in movement	0.246	-0.128**
F-2. Powerlessness	0.373	-0.195**
F-3. Unusually strong gastrointestinal function	0.168	-0.088*
Psychological Factors		
P-1. Dissatisfaction	0.003	-0.018
P-2. Lifelessness	0.239	-0.127**
P-3. Fragility	0.278	-0.147**

*p<0.05, **p<0.01.

Differentiating factors

Based on the results of the *t*-test of means of obtained factor scores of schizophrenic and normal control groups, five proved to be factors that differentiated the two groups. These factors are F-1 (dullness in movement, t=3.099, df=159.101, p=0.002), F-2 (powerlessness, t=4.458, df=136.065, p=0.000), F-3 (unusually strong gastrointestinal function, t=2.332, df=263, p=0.020), P-2 (lifelessness, t=3.042,df=260, p=0.003) and P-3 (fragility, t=4.507, df=260, p=0.000). (See Table 4.)

Related Clinical Characteristics

Symptoms

The results of the *t*-test of differentiating factor scores between schizophrenic subgroups composed of SAPS and SANS scores are shown in Table 5. The high-score (>5.28) group on hallucinations (SAPS-1) showed a statistically significantly higher factor score on F-2 (powerlessness, t=2.567, df=89, p=0.012) and P-2 (lifelessness, t=2.426, df=89, p=0.017) than the low-score group. The high-score (>10.12) group on delusions (SAPS-2) showed a statistically significantly higher factor score on F-2 (powerlessness, t=2.100, df=89, p=0.039) and P-2 (lifelessness, t=3.814, df=89, p=0.000) than the low-score group.

Table 5. Differential BIQ factor scores in high and low score groups of SAPS and SANS. (Study 1)

	Positive symptoms		Negative symptoms	
	SAPS		SANS	
Factors	High	LOW	High	LOW
	SAPS-1		SANS-1	
	Hallucinations		Affective flattening or blunting	
F-1	–	–	–	–
F-2	0.789	0.178*	–	–
F-3	–	–	–	–
P-2	0.608	0.058*	–	–
P-3	–	–	–	–
	SAPS-2		SANS-2	
	Delusions		Alogia	
F-1	–	–	–	–
F-2	0.708	0.208*	–	–
F-3	–	–	–	–
P-2	0.794	-0.033**	–	–
P-3	–	–	–	–
	SAPS-3		SANS-3	
	Bizarre Behaviour		Avolition Apathy	
F-1	–	–	–	–
F-2	–	–	0.805	-0.013**
F-3	–	–	–	–
P-2	–	–	–	–
P-3	–	–	–	–
	SAPS-4		SANS-4	
	Positive formal Thought Disorder		Anhedonia-associality	
F-1	–	–	–	–
F-2	0.723	0.098**	0.718	0.064**
F-3	–	–	–	–
P-2	–	–	0.599	-0.082**
P-3	–	–	–	–
	SAPS-5		SANS-5	
	Inappropriate affect		Attention	
F-1	–	–	–	–
F-2	–	–	–	–
F-3	–	–	–	–
	SAPS		SANS	
P-2	–	–	–	–
P-3	–	–	–	–
	SAPS-Total		SANS-Total	
F-1	–	–	–	–
F-2	.729	0.180*	–	–
F-3	–	–	–	–
P-2	0.556	0.067*	–	–
P-3	–	–	–	–

High =High score group. Low=Low score group. *=p<0.05, **=p<0.01.

The high-score (>8.96) group on positive formal thought disorder (SAPS-4) showed a statistically significantly higher factor score on F-2 (powerlessness, t=2.819, df=89, p=0.006) than the low-score group. The high-score (>26.2) group on total SAPS showed a statistically significantly higher factor score on F-2 (powerlessness, t=2.358, df=89, p=0.021) and P-2 (lifelessness, t=2.175, df=89, p=0.032) than the low-score group.

The high-score (>12.2) group on avolition-apathy (SANS-3) showed a statistically significantly higher factor score on F-2 (powerlessness, t=3.852, df=89, p=0.000) than the low-score group. The high-score (>13.7) group on anhedonia-asociality (SANS-4) showed a statistically significantly higher factor score on F-2 (powerlessness, t=2.983, df=89, p=0.004) and P-2 (lifelessness, t=3.272, df=89, p=0.002) than the low-score group.

Insight

The results of the *t*-test of differentiating factor scores between schizophrenic subgroups composed of SAI scores are shown in Table 6. The high-score (>3.29) group on acceptance (SAI-1) showed a statistically significantly lower factor score on F-3 (unusually strong digestive function, t=-2.482, df=89, p=0.015) and higher factor score on P-3 (Fragility, t=2.135, df=89, p=0.036) than the low-score group. The high-score (>1.7) group on hypothetical contradiction (SAI-supplement) showed a statistically significantly lower factor score on F-3 (unusually strong gastrointestinal function, t=-2.348, df=89, p=0.021) than the low-score group.

Table 6. Differential BIQ factor scores in high and low score groups of SAI. (Study 1)

BIQ	SAI		SAI	
Factors	High	Low	High	Low
	SAI-1a.		SAI-1b.	
	Treatment compliance (passive)		Treatment compliance (unprompted)	
F-1	–	–	–	–
F-2	–	–	–	–
F-3	0.047	0.546*	–	–
P-2	–	–	–	–
P-3	0.368	-0.059*	–	–

Table 6. (Continued)

BIQ	SAI		SAI	
Factors	High	Low	High	Low
	SAI-2a.		SAI-2b.	
	Awareness of illness		Awareness of illness	
	(mental, physical)		(mental, psychiatric)	
F-1	–	–	–	–
F-2	–	–	–	–
F-3	–	–	–	–
P-2	–	–	–	–
P-3	–	–	–	–
	SAI-2c.			
	Explanation of illness			
F-1	–	–		
F-2	–	–		
F-3	–	–		
P-2	–	–		
P-3	–	–		
	SAI-3a.		SAI-3b.	
	Relabelling		Explanation	
	of psychotic experience		of psychotic experience	
F-1	–	–	–	–
F-2	–	–	–	–
F-3	–	–	–	–
P-2	–	–	–	–
P-3	–	–	–	–
	SAI-total		SAI-supplemental	
			Hypothetical Contradiction	
F-1	–	–	–	–
F-2	–	–	–	–
F-3	–	–	-0.135	0.303*
P-2	–	–	–	–
P-3	–	–	–	–

*=$p<0.05$.

Other Clinical Characteristics

There was no significant difference between subgroups of body image factor scores in years of hospitalization, age at onset of disease or the daily chlorpromazine-equivalent dose.

Discussion

The factor analysis identified five differentiating factors, which showed that there is body image aberration in schizophrenic patients: dullness in movement, powerlessness, unusually strong digestive function, lifelessness and fragility. These findings, along with those of other investigations (Roehricht and Priebe, 1996; Coleman et al., 1996; Chapman LJ, Chapman and Raulin, 1978), revealed that schizophrenics manifested perceptual and cognitive deficits in body image.

Among the five differential body image factors, only two factors showed correlation with positive symptoms measured by SAPS: powerlessness and lifelessness, and the same factors correlated with negative symptoms. These results highlighted the close relationships between powerless and lifeless body images and severity in symptoms, both positive and negative, implying that the patients with severe symptoms would have powerless and lifeless body images.

Although the current view is that schizophrenics lack insight (Amador et al. 1994, 1991,; Cuesta and Peralta, 1994), the results of the present study showed that there is variation in degree of insight measured by SAI. The results also showed that acceptance of treatment, as one component of insight, as assessed by the SAI, proved to be related negatively with unusual gastrointestinal function and positively with the fragile body image, showing that patients who comply with treatment have fragile body images and have images of digestive organs that are not too strong. It might be well estimated that the fragile body image and the reduction of strength of images of digestive organs enhance the patients' feeling of needing help, which makes them compliant to treatment. Another insight component that showed a relationship with the deviated body image factor was the double-awareness phase, as assessed by the hypothetical contradiction, a supplemental item of the SAI. This was conceived as the degree of the patient's conviction about the delusion, as it appeared in the recovery from delusion (Sacks et al, 1974), and arising "from rapid oscillations between belief and disbelief." The score suggests "the amenability to test still firmly held beliefs against reality" (Sacks et al, 1974). The degree of double awareness was shown to be inversely related with the image of unusual strength of gastrointestinal function, showing that the patients with flexible amenability to delusional ideas have images of digestive organs that are not very strong.

The overall results proved two out of the five factors that differentiated the schizophrenic from the normal group to be related to positive and negative symptoms and two to insight. It is important that one major differentiating factor, dullness in movement, did not show any correlation with symptoms or insight. During the 1990s, observations focused on the fact that while patients' symptoms were improved markedly by antipsychotic agents, the patients still required assisted living arrangements and could not work in highly competitive situations (Goldberg et al, 1993). The fact that the main part of the body image deviancy assessed by BIQ did not relate to positive or negative symptoms is assumed to have some relation to these observations, and suggests the possibility that the main component of body image deviancy, which is independent from severity of symptoms, is closely related to some deficits that are germane to schizophrenia.

Conclusion

The factor analysis of BIQ showed some aberrant phases of schizophrenics' body image. They were: dullness in movement, powerlessness, unusually strong gastrointestinal function, lifelessness and fragility. Powerlessness and lifelessness proved to be related to positive and negative symptoms and unusually strong gastrointestinal functions and fragility, to insight.

Study 2. Schizophrenics' Body Images: | What are They?

Introduction

In Study 1, the attempts with factor analysis to find out the linkage of schizophrenics' aberrant body image with clinical characteristics proved to be exhaustive. However, the results of factor analysis showed that there are some differential body image factors, none of which seemed to relate to an anatomical component of body image of schizophrenia. It was further observed that most of the BIQ differential items were functional and psychological.

Distorted body experiences in schizophrenic patients, especially regarding their images of their body shape or proportions, have been reported since the 1960s. DeLeon et al (1989) denoted dysmorphophobia as a symptom which occurs in a number of different disorders, notably in schizophrenia. Dysmorphophobia as seen in somatoform disorders (1980), body dysmorphic disorder (1987) and delusional disorder, somatic subtype, were included in the Diagnostic and Statistical Manual of Mental Disorders, which produced considerable concern about delusion regarding the appearance of the body. (deLeon et al, 1989; Phillips et al, 1994). There has also been much discussion on distorted body experiences, which are legitimately categorized as psychological derivative imageries, including coenaesthesis (Huber, 1957; Rohricht and Priebe, 1996; Schmoll, 1994). Much concern has been placed on the blurred nature of body boundaries (Quinlan and Harrow, 1974; Fisher S, 1966), and the Rorschach test has been used to examine the vulnerable characteristics of body boundaries such as penetrability. In spite of all these attempts, clinical relevance of body image aberration remains unclear. It is still uncertain whether or not the body images are deviated in the area of visual imagery, or in feelings about their body such as being hard as stone or being fragile.

Thus, the question of which phase of body image links with symptoms and which to recovery? leads to the next question, "What are schizophrenics' body images, or what are their aberrations?" In this section, attempts were made to clarify this question simply by comparing three hypothetical components of BIQ, that is, anatomical, functional, and psychological, between schizophrenic and non-schizophrenic groups.

Method

Assessment of Body Image Deviation

Body images were assessed using the BIQ. The three BIQ component scores, *anatomical, functional,* and *psychological,* were obtained using scoring system with reverse items. (See, Appendix 1-1.) Items included in each component are shown in the Appendix. (See Appendix 1-3, 1-4 and 1-5.)

Subjects

The study sample consisted of 83 chronic schizophrenics; 44 were men and 39 were women. The mean (SD) age of the patients was 48.2 (10.0) years. All of them were inpatients in chronic psychiatric wards of a mental hospital in Ibaraki Prefecture in Japan. They were diagnosed as schizophrenia, according to DSM-IV criteria (Subtypes: 20 Paranoid types, 36 Disorganized types, 23 Residual types, 4 Undifferentiated types). The mean (SD) duration of hospitalization was 23.7 (10.5) years, and the mean (SD) age of onset was 24.2 (7.0) years old. Their mean (SD) dose of neuroleptics was 437.0 (396.9) mg/day of chrolpromazine equivalent dose. The group with anxiety disorders was comprised of 43 patients with anxiety disorders in DSM-IV, including 23 men and 20 women. They were outpatients of a private clinic in Ibaraki Prefecture in Japan. The mean (SD) age was 39.1 (14.1) years old. The normal control group of study 1 was used. All of the study participants were informed of the purpose of the study and actively participated with a written informed consent. (See Table 7.)

Table 7. Demographic and clinical characteristics of subjects. (Study 2)

	Schizophrenia	Anxiety Disorders	Normals
	(N=83)	(N=43)	N=177
Demographic characteristics			
Mean Age	48.2	39.1	44.9
Gender (Male %)	53.0	53.4	44.0
Clinical characteristics of the schizophrenic patients			
	Mean (Range)		
Age of Onset	24.2 (14-45)		
Years of Hospitalization	23.7 (3-47)		
Dose of CPZ (mg/day)	437.0 (30-1256)		

Data Analysis

Means of the three BIQ component scores were compared among groups with schizophrenia, anxiety disorders and normals using ANOVA, followed by multiple comparisons using the Tukey method. The means of each item score of the differential component scores obtained were compared between the schizophrenic and non-schizophrenic groups using ANOVA.

Results

The results of ANOVA are shown in Table 8, and the results of succeeded multiple comparisons are shown in Table 12. Statistically significant group differences in means were found in the BIQ functional component score ($F=12.478$, $df=2/284$, $p=0.000$). Further multiple comparisons of differences of means showed a statistically significant difference between groups with schizophrenia and anxiety disorders ($p=0.021$), and between groups with schizophrenia and normal groups ($p = 0.000$). There was no statistically significant difference among the three diagnostic groups in the BIQ anatomical component score or in the BIQ psychological component score.

Table 8. Group means of BIQ component Scores. (Study 2)

	Schizophrenia	Anxiety Disorders	Normals	
	(N=83)	(N=43)	(N=177)	F
Anatomical	80.6	70.71	79.1	1.818
Functional	78.4	73.07	71.4	12.478***
Psychological	78.4	84.77	72.5	2.800
Total	238.8	228.34	223.1	18.046***

*P<0.05, **P<0.01, ***P<0.001.

The mean scores of BIQ functional items, which composed the differential component, were further compared between schizophrenic and non-schizophrenic groups. Eight out of 17 items showed statistically significant differences, including being weak (F=7.262, df=2, p<.001), being liable to get sick (F=10.810, df=2, p<.000), moving slowly (F=6.065, df=2, p<.003), being poor at athletics (F=7.743, df=2, p<.001),, being liable to lose balance(F=5.092, df=2, p<.007), walking slowly(F=3.314, df=2, p<.038), being unable to work in dark rooms(F=10.415, df=2, p<.000), and having weak teeth (F=5.614, df=2, p<.004). The means of each functional item are shown in Table 9.

Table 9. Means of BIQ-Functional items of three diagnostic groups. (Study 2)

	SC	AD	NO	F
01. My body is weak.	3.853	3.558	3.175	7.264***
03. I often get sick.	3.734	3.558	2.945	10.810***
09. I move slowly.	4.253	3.857	3.649	6.065**
13. I am good at athletics.®	4.465	4.432	3.626	7.743**
17. I often lose my balance.	3.790	3.566	3.153	5.092**
21. I walk slowly.	4.409	3.690	4.101	3.314*
37. I can work well in dark rooms. ®	3.570	3.418	2.783	10.415***
47. My teeth are weak.	4.817	4.209	4.079	5.614**

®=reverse item.

*P<0.05, **P<0.01, ***P<0.001.

Discussion

Results of this study showed aberration restricted to functional imageries, revealing that there are both intact and deficient phases in schizophrenics' body images. Of three hypothesized components, that is, anatomical, functional, and psychological body images, only functional imageries proved to be deviant.

The results of the comparisons of means of the various functional items between groups showed that differences included three categories of ill-functional body imageries. First was vulnerability to illness, including images of being weak and of being liable to get sick. Second was difficulty in manipulating their bodies, including images of being unable to work in dark rooms, being poor at athletics, walking slowly and of moving slowly. The third category was unusual concern over gastrointestinal functions reflected in having weak teeth.

Conclusion

Via the analysis of three hypothetical components of BIQ, the schizophrenic body image deviation proved to be comprised of deviation in functional imageries.

Study 3. Depression and Body Image in Chronic Schizophrenia

Introduction

Although mood disorders are conventionally viewed as nosologically distinct from schizophrenia, depression in schizophrenia has been recognized from the time of Mayer-Gross (1920) and Bleuler (1911/1950). Comorbid depressive signs and symptoms (DSS) in schizophrenia were earlier described as postpsychotic depression (McGlaschan and Carpenter, 1976), resulting from realization of disability once psychosis has abated and insight is recovered. A second view is described as post-treatment depression in which neuroleptic medication causes depression in schizophrenia (Van Puttan and May, 1978 ;Galdi, 1983). The concept has been further elaborated by Van Putten and May (1978), who argued that depression in schizophrenia might be specifically associated with extrapyramidal side effects of neuroleptic medication. A third view relates depression to the schizophrenic process itself. According to this hypothesis, depression forms an integral part of the illness, predicting that depressive symptoms would be most prevalent during the acute phase of illness and subside with treatment (Knights and Hirsch, 1981; Hirsch, 1982).

Recently, DSS have become a target of treatment because novel antipsychotic agents introduce new avenues that may differentially affect schizophrenic signs and symptoms, including depression (Pickar, 1995; Tollefson et al., 1998), and its association with a higher risk of suicide and self-harm (Siris, 1991; Hu et al., 1991; Drake and Cotton, 1986; Caldwell and Gottesman, 1990; Cohen et al., 1990; Roy et al., 1983) has been highlighted. There are studies that reported depressive schizophrenics attempt at unusual self-mutilation (Feldman, 1988; Burgess, 1991; Martin and Gattaz, 1991; Weiser et al., 1993; Kennedy and Feldmann, 1994), which suggest a close relationship between DSS in schizophrenia to body image aberrations.

The report in this section looks at depression in schizophrenia by detecting its unique relationship to patients' body image using BIQ.

Method

Subjects

The subjects in study 1 were used. (See Table 1.)

Assessment of Depression

Depression was assessed by Zung's Self-rating Depression Scale (SDS, Zung, 1965). The SDS scores ranged from 24 to 64, and their mean (SD) was 40.0 (7.9). Based on the distribution, the (schizophrenic and normal) depressive groups were comprised of those who scored 48 or higher, which included 20.3% of all subjects, including schizophrenicc and normal populations. The non-depressive groups were comprised of those who scored 32 or lower, which included 18.9% of all subjects.

Data Analysis

The means of the factor scores obtained in study 1 were compared between the depressive (SDS scores >=48) and non-depressive (SDS scores =<32) groups in schizophrenic and normal control samples, respectively, using *t*-tests. In addition, 59 item scores of BIQ were compared between high and low score groups in these comparative sets using *t*-tests.

Results

Based on the results of the *t*-test of means of obtained factor scores of schizophrenic depressive and non-depressive groups, 5 of these proved to be factors that differentiated the two groups. These factors and their interpretations are factor A-3 (roundness, t=-2.420, df=37, p=0.021), factor F-2 (powerlessness, t=2.407, df=38, p=0.021), factor F-3(Unusually strong gastrointestinal function, t=-2.588, df=38, p=0.014), factor P-1 (Dissatisfuction, t=2.491, df=38, p=0.015) and factor P-2 (Lifelessness, t=2.556, df=38, p=0.015). Among these factors, significant differences were found among normal population in factor P-1 (t= 5.010, df=40, p=0.000), and factor P-2 (t=2.756, df=40, p=0.009), showing that schizophrenic and normal groups had common relationships of depression to body image along with these factors. The other three of the five factors did not differentiate depressive and non-depressive groups in normal samples. Also, there was no factor differentiating depressive and non-depressive group uniquely found in the normal samples. (See Table 10.)

Table 10. BIQ Factors differentiating depressive and non-depressive state. (Study 3)

Factors	Schizophrenic		Control	
	D	Non-D	D	Non-D
A-1	_	_	_	_
A-2	_	_	_	_
A-3	-2.220	.449*	_	_
F-1	_	_	_	_
F-2	.794	-.030*	_	_
F-3	-.165	.620*	_	_
P-1	.262	-.513*	.764	-.331***
P-2	.751	-.198*	.411	-.356*
P-3	_	_	_	_

D=Depressive group, Non-D=Non-depressive group. *P<.0.05, **P<0.01, ***P<0.001.

There were BIQ items which differentiated depressive and non-depressive groups only in schizophrenic samples. These were; having small eyes, being not meager, being weak, being clumsy with hands, having unusually strong stomach, having strong heart, having strong bowels, being underdeveloped, feeling cold, being dissatisfied, not minding being touched by others, and being getting worse. Schizophrenic and normal control samples shared the most of the differentiating items in the psychological element. (See table 11.)

Table 11. BIQ items differentiating depressive and non-depressive state. (Study 3)

BIQ items	Schizophrenics		Normals	
	D	Non-D	D	Non-D
Anatomical				
18. I have small eyes.	4.200	3.181*		
44. My body is not meager.®	4.266	3.000**		
Functional				
01. My body is weak.	4.600	3.454*		
03. I often get sick.	4.400	3.000*	3.461	2.655*
17. I often lose my balance.			4.461	2.714***
25. I am clumsy with my hands.	4.833	3.181**		
37. I can work well in dark rooms. ®	5.666	4.181**	3.692	4.655*
38. My stomach is not unusually strong. ®	3.600	5.181**		
42. My heart is strong. ®	3.933	2.272**		
53. My bowels are unusually strong.	3.766	5.000*		
Psychological				
06. My body is underdeveloped.	3.866	2.636*		
07. My body is clean.®			3.153	2.413**
10. My body is defective.	4.400	3.363*	4.692	3.448**
11. My body feels cold.	4.233	5.363*		
12. My body is beautiful.®	4.333	3.272*	4.769	3.482***
22. I seldom feel tired.®			5.461	4.206**
23. My mood is numb.	3.833	5.090*	2.000	4.724***
27. I am satisfied with my body. ®	3.200	4.727*		
31. I am always cheerful. ®			3.923	2.931**
32. My body is unattractive.			5.153	3.931***
34. I always feel sick.	4.433	3.181*	4.615	3.413***
BIQ items	D	Non-D	D	Non-D
43. I don't mind being touched by others. ®	4.866	3.636*		
45. I seldom get excited			2.833	4.275**
46. My health is getting better. ®	5.000	3.900*		
49. I am seldom tense.	2.400	3.909**	2.076	3.241**
59. I always feel energetic.®	4.666	3.363**	4.307	3.137**

D=Depressive group, Non-D=Non-depressive group. *P<.0.05, **P<0.01, ***P<0.001.

Discussion

The depression assessed by SDS correlated to 5 factors of body image assessed by BIQ. The findings further demonstrated that 3 among these 5 factors correlated with depression in schizophrenic groups, interpreted as roundness, dullness in movement, and unusually strong gastrointestinal function, none of which differentiated depressive from non-depressive group in normal subjects. It would be reasonable to assume that there is some close link between depression and body image, which is unique and specific to schizophrenia.

Dissatisfied and lifeless body images were found to be related to depression in schizophrenic as well as in normal samples. Dissatisfaction and lifelessness would be a common body image factors they shared regardless of diagnosis. In the schizophrenic sample, three differentiating factors were further observed, one anatomical factor, and two functional factors. It was observed that the more the schizophrenic patients becomes depressed, the less round and the less powerful their imagined body becomes and that the more they depressed, the less powerful their gastrointestinal function becomes in their body images. The results of the comparisons of means of each BIQ item also demonstrated that the variety of functional body image items differentiated depressive from non-depressive patients in the schizophrenic sample. The concern on bodily function proved to be prominent in schizophrenic depressive patients.

These observations may suggest that these depression-related body images in schizophrenia have characteristics, which lead to the anticipation of the serious corporeal deterioration of becoming immovable. This close linkage between depression and undesirable functional body images in schizophrenic patients would be connected with the self-mutilation or higher risk of self-harm observed in schizophrenia.

Chapter 3

STUDIES USING RORSCHACH TEST: SUBSIDIARY FINDINGS

STUDY 4. A UNIQUE RORSCHACH RESPONSE OBSERVED IN SCHIZOPHRENIC PATIENTS

Introduction

Although recognized as closely linked with psychopathology, distortion of body image has seldom been studied in schizophrenia. The major cause of the neglect of this concept is methodological, i.e., the difficulty in developing assessment techniques. In this section, a new finding concerning body image of schizophrenia, as observed in their Rorschach responses, is reported.

In the attempts to detect body image aberration in the studies using the BIQ, we found that responses that evoke images of a mass of flesh are often seen in schizophrenic Rorschach responses. This was first noticed in the response of a schizophrenic patient (Case A of this study) as "This looks like a mass of flesh of some kind of animal, though I cannot specify which," to Card VI. This response followed to the failure to construct the response "a gorilla" in Card IV, in which she could not identify its legs, arms, or head. According to this Rorschach sequence, a process is assumed to exist in schizophrenic thought that the their bodies are becoming a mere mass of flesh, as if they were being vivisected though still alive, which forms a core of fear of schizophrenic patients. Difficulty in identifying legs, arms, and head of perceived animals or human beings also proved to be a process of perceiving "a mass of flesh."

Starting with these observations, an attempt was made to explore similar responses in schizophrenics' Rorschach responses, and it was found that these responses are quite common in schizophrenic patients. We call the characteristics revealed in these responses as body image "becoming a mass of flesh" and present the hypothesis that this might form a core characteristic of body image of schizophrenia.

Responses such as "mass of flesh", or "muscles in the shoulder of a man," are typical mass of flesh responses because the image of a mass of flesh is clearly verbalized in these responses. Responses such as "a rat without legs" or "a girl, but I cannot see her hands" are also mass-of-flesh responses, because these responses, though indirect, vaguely imagine a mass of flesh through the diminution of head, legs, and arms and emphasis on the trunk.

Four cases are presented. All of them were inpatients of a chronic care ward of a mental hospital in Ibaraki Prefecture and were diagnosed as schizophrenia according to DSM-IV. All patients were informed of the purpose of the study and actively participated with written informed consent. The socio-demographic and clinical characteristics, such as illness type, onset age, years of hospitalization, BPRS scores (Overall and Gorham, 1962), and daily dose of neuroleptics, are shown in Table 12.

Table 12. Demographic and clinical characteristics of subjects. (Study 4)

	Case A	Case B	Case C	Case D
Age	62	46	33	28
Gender	Female	Female	Male	Female
Years of education	9	7	13	12
Years of employment	2	0	0	4
Illnessl types	Paranoid	Disorganized	Disorganized	Residual
Age at onset	19	16	19	22
Years of hospitalization	37	30	33	5
BPRS	51	49	64	25
Daily dose of neuroleptics (mg)	400	1525	175	350

Case Reports

Case A

Miss A was a 62-year-old woman. She was born to a farmer in Ibaraki Prefecture in Japan as the first of seven children. After she graduated from high school, she went to Tokyo and worked as a housekeeper, but one year later she became restless, sleepless, and went back home. At the age of 22, she was admitted to the hospital with prominent delusional experiences. She left the hospital once, but soon left home, wandered around, stole food from a store and was returned the hospital. Since then, she has been in the hospital for 37 years.

In a semi-structured interview, she said, "A fox is controlling me. He exchanges my body with that of a victim of a traffic accident, so that I feel great pain in my legs, head, and arms. The fox is one of the foxes I keep at home. He changes my body because he gets money through traffic accidents. I am a splendid and super woman. If I had not been ill, I would have made a country. I sculpted on the moon as well as the sun."

In the Rorschach Test, she gave one response per card and gave in seven responses among ten animals with unclear or absent legs, arms, or head, or irregular emphasis on the legs. "Two elephants, but the legs are too short for elephants"(Card II). "A bat, legs are just like those of a bat" (Card V). "An animal I have never seen before. It looks like a gorilla, but this has no head, no legs, and no arms" (Card IV, IX). "A shrimp, with big tails and many small legs"(Card IX).

Case B

Miss B was a 46-year-old woman. She was a third of four children in the family of a public official. She suffered from tuberculosis in the junior high school. One day she was made a fun of by her classmates and refused to go to school. At the age of sixteen, she began to speak in monologues and to spend almost all day in bed. She showed delusions and hallucinations, and entered into the hospital when she was seventeen years old.

In the interview, she said, "I have been suffering from hallucinations everyday for twenty or thirty years. I hear the voice of a middle-aged woman, and she always says bad things about me. It causes severe pain in my shoulder. But I still continue knitting. When I brush my teeth, I feel like I am dying. When I am in bed, and also I am walking, germs move and frighten me, and dogs and cats are lying on me. All animals are transparent so that I cannot see them but they certainly exist."

She presented feelings of "being pressed" in 3 responses among a total of 7. "A calf oppressed by a fixed butterfly" (Card II). "Human beings are pressed down with their hands on the floor" (Card III). "A crab which is compressed, narrow in width" (Card X). She also showed an image of becoming a mass in the response, "A rat, there are no legs" to Card VIII.

Case C

Mr. C was a 55-year-old man. He was born the fourth child of a wealthy family in Tokyo. His father owned a company, and he went to private school. When he was in university, in the first year, he went to a supermarket with the group of his friends to steal some small things. He was expelled from the university. Since then, he complained of anxiety at meeting people, and visited many clinics for medication and psychotherapy, but he gradually came to stay at home almost all day. When he was 22 years old, he entered the hospital with prominent delusions and hallucinations.

In the interview, the patient said, "I suffer from nightmares every night. It is a dream of hell and I feel I cannot survive any more with these ominous ideas. I cannot concentrate. I am slow in thinking. And I have become old-fashioned. Somebody is talking ill of me. I feel suspected as a criminal every time a crime is broadcast on the television. It is because I know the names of the criminals, so that this is my referential delusion."

He showed five human movement responses, none of which identified the agent. "Hitting each other with both hands" (Card I), "Washing" (Card III), "Dancing" (Card VI), "Being astonished (Card VII), and "Talking, with each other" (Card X). He also showed over-clarification of ages in his human percepts, as "old" (Card II), "middle-aged" (Cards III, X), and "young" (Card VII). These estimations of age without evidence suggest the possibility that there might be strong conflict in his subjective inability to experience time, from which he feels excluded.

Case D

Miss D is a 28-year-old woman. She was the second of two children of a family of an artisan in Ibaraki Prefecture. When she was 16 years old, she felt that her classmates are talking ill of her so she refused to go to school. She once consulted with a psychologist. After she graduated from high school, she went to Tokyo and worked for a large company there for five years. When her mother got sick, she came back home to see her mother. Soon after her mother died, she became sleepless, violent especially toward her father, suffered from hallucinations and entered the hospital at the age of 23. After her admission, the hallucinations disappeared, and she returned home to stay several times, although she was not successful in staying home every time because of her violent behaviour toward her father.

In the interview, she said, "I feel miserable because I am under the protection of my father who is so slovenly that he spends a lot of money on bicycle races. My father hit me. But it is because I poured water on him. I am worried that I cannot be independent, though I am old enough to be. To tell the truth, I want to be a child of my elder sister."

She presented the body image as a mass of flesh in the response, "A crab, with torso with a carapace and nippers" (Card III), in which the mass-of-flesh image was covered with the hard shield of a crab and the impression of the whole response was aggressive and defensive, ready for fight. She also showed withdrawal of the body from the outer world in the response, "A piece of clothing, too showy for me." She showed helpless feelings in the response, "A flower, with leaves hanging down and connected with the roots in this way" (Card IX). In this response, the psychological process is presented as a feeling of helplessness that was developed into an attempt to confirm that she was related to her support system.

Discussion

The body image becoming a mass of flesh was seen in four cases as a common characteristics of body image, regardless of their variety of illness type, of degree of severity of symptoms assessed by BPRS, life history and daily dose of neuroleptic medication. Clarification of how this mass-of-flesh image is expressed and is related to the patients' clinical pictures is necessary. Three questions need to be discussed with regard to these patients: (1) Is mass-of-flesh image really related to delusion?: (2) Is it related to hallucinatory behaviour? (3) Is it related to symptoms other than delusional and hallucinatory experiences?

Case A refers to the first question. In this case, body image as a mass of flesh was expressed in a typical form as "a mass of flesh of some animal with a bamboo stick." From this response, it is assumed that she has a catastrophic fear of her body being exposed to the outer world without protection, being penetrated. It is further guessed that this fear is elaborated into a delusional belief to clarify and explain its origin, by thinking that a naughty fox exchanged her body with that of a victim of a traffic accident, and that the fox is one of many foxes she kept at home.

Case B exemplifies to the second question. In this case, the body image of becoming a mass of flesh was expressed as "a rat without arms and legs" and also as "a crab which was compressed" and "a calf that was oppressed by a butterfly." These responses imply that body image as becoming a mass of flesh modified into more sensory form as "being pressed" and developed into a hallucination. She suffered from being oppressed at shoulder presumably caused by a middle-aged woman's voice. She also suffered from being oppressed by germs creeping on her and by transparent animals lying on her.

Case C refers to the third question. In this case, the agents in human Rorschach percepts are frequently not identified. Omission of the head is an indirect expression of body image as a mass of flesh. The lack of identification of the agents of the human percepts implies his avoidance of committing himself to the percepts. With this withdrawal, he tries to maintain distance by regarding the whole situation in which he lives as if it were a fiction, acted on a stage, and regarding himself as an audience. He described his own symptoms as “referential delusion” as if others observe him and felt himself “like a criminal who appears on television”. His over-concern about age and many attempts to guess age without enough evidence would be derived phenomenon from this withdrawal from the real world, in which time passes, into a fictional narcissistic world, in which there is no lapse of time. He is worried about “becoming old-fashioned.” This concern toward age seems consistent with the age-disorientation of schizophrenia (Crow and Johnstone, 1980; Crow and Stevens, 1978). It was reported that 25% of the schizophrenic patients mistake their own ages by more than 5 years.

In Case D, the mass-of-flesh percepts appeared in the perception, “A crab, with a torso with a carapace and nippers” (Card III). A mass of flesh was seen in the elimination of the legs with armor. This is consistent with her clinical picture, in which her violent acting-out is a prominent problem. As the risk of violence has come to be one of the current issues of schizophrenia (Taylor, 1995; Fottrell,1980; Humphreys et al., 1992) the present finding seems to relate to some illness-specific risk factor to evoke violence in schizophrenic patients. In this case, it is assumed that an “armored mass-of-flesh body image” would be a compromised product of an aggressive premorbid personality and schizophrenic illness.

The body image as becoming a mass of flesh is considered to have four connotations. First, it suggests an image of the body, which is still alive, though exposed to the outer world. Second, it suggests an image of the body that is helplessly threatened and unprotected. Third, it suggests an image of the body that is unmovable. Fourth, it suggests an image of the body that is weakened and helpless. These would constitute an image of potential catastrophe concerning the patients’ own body.

The image of becoming a mass of flesh was recognized in two stages. Stage 1 is presented directly with reference to “a mass of muscles” or “mass of flesh,” as seen as a typical response one. Stage 2 as presented indirectly as an animal or a human being without legs or arms, or without clarifying them, in which the mass of flesh is vaguely imagined through the diminution of head or legs. In observation of these four cases above, stage 1 presumably works with delusion, especially being closely linked with bizarre delusions and enhancing psychological factors for it. Stage 2 would exist as a rather general, though underlying, disposition in schizophrenic patients. In the case of stage 2, it was further shown that image of becoming a mass of flesh leads to some readiness for age-disorientation as one of the major thought disorders, as well as violent acting-out behaviours, so that one of the future topics to be discussed should be the effect of the image of becoming a mass of flesh on the formation of a variety of schizophrenic symptoms.

Conclusion

Rorschach responses that imply the body images of becoming a mass of flesh were shown in four chronic schizophrenic cases. The body images of becoming a mass of flesh were experienced in two forms: one is experienced by the percept of a mass of muscles. The other is by percepts of an animal or a human being with diminished legs, head, or arms. In studying four cases carefully, these responses were found regardless of the illness type, duration of illness, life history, and neuroleptic doses, but they related not only to delusional and hallucinatory symptoms but also to some other thought disorders such as age-disorientation as well as violence. Because this is just an initial phase of the study, further studies are required to determine whether this finding is a general intrinsic trend of schizophrenia or not.

Study 5. A Mass of Flesh: Schizophrenic Rorschach Percepts

Introduction

The Rorschach test is important in the diagnosis of schizophrenia. Since 1966, 1728 studies using the Rorschach test, among which 126 were concerned with the diagnosis of schizophrenia, have been indexed in Medline. Rorschach protocols have been documented in thought disorders, sometimes in terms of ego impairment, to provide information concerning diagnosis of schizophrenia. Rappaport et al. (1968) are historically credited with systematically identifying deviant aspects of the patient's verbal responses to the inkblot. Attempts have been made to develop specific criteria on the Rorschach designed to make a more accurate assessment of thought disorders, including the Delta Index (Watkins and Stauffacher, 1952), Thought Disorder Index (Johnston and Holzman, 1979), and Schizophrenia Index (Exner, 1974, 1978, 1986a, 1986b, 1991, 1993; Mason et al., 1985). Earlier, methods were developed to assess "primary process" manifestations (Holt, 1977; Meloy, 1984) or boundary disturbance manifestations (Quinlan and Harrow, 1974). During the 1970s to 1980s, methods to assess object relations were developed to differentiate borderline personality disorders from schizophrenia (Urist, 1977; Kwawer, 1980). In the 1990s, Wagner and Frye (Wagner and Frye, 1990) reported the diagnostic implication of the "fragmented" Rorschach W:D (Whole Responses vs. Detail Responses) ratio in schizophrenia, and Perry developed perseveration measures (Perry and Braff, 1998). One of the most widely used of these Rorschach criteria for the evaluation of schizophrenia is the Comprehensive System's Schizophrenia Indices, SCZI (Exner, 1974; Mason et al., 1985). The Comprehensive System began to pay more attention to the importance of systematically measuring unusual verbalizations and identifying reliable test signs that capture a range of aberrations in thought and language. The diagnostic indicators of disordered thinking in Exner's approach pointed to large differences between schizophrenia and control subjects, confirming an impairment of perceptual accuracy, reality testing and reduced emotional control (Di-Nuovo et al., 1988), and the Exner Rorschach was judged to be a valid test for schizophrenia (Vincent and Harman, 1991; Hilsenroth et al., 1998). Another index, the Ego Impairment Index, proved to differentiate among schizophrenics according to the severity of their ego impairment (Perry et al., 1992). Recently, investigators have placed much emphasis on Rorschach indications for thought disorders in regard to sensorimotor gating abnormalities or other information processing in the neurocognitive context (Perry and Braff, 1994; Perry et al., 1999).

In the previous section (study 4), a new finding was reported concerning Rorschach percepts of schizophrenia, that images of a mass of flesh were often seen in schizophrenic Rorschach responses. This was first noticed in the Rorschach response to Card VI of a middle-aged female (Case A) with chronic schizophrenia in the statement, "This looks like a mass of flesh of some kind of animal, although I cannot specify which animal." Before producing this response, the patient had failed to make the response of " a gorilla" to Card IV, in which she could not identify its arms, legs or head. According to these Rorschach sequences, it would be considered that if the patient has failed to see the legs and arms, a gorilla is perceived as a mass of flesh. A similar response was found in another middle-aged male with chronic schizophrenia, who responded to Card IX, "Part of a naked man, the swelling muscles of his shoulder." This patient also responded to Card VIII, "The carcass of an animal. Only bones here, for the flesh is gone." In this response, he imagined a mass of flesh and quickly eliminated it by thinking of it as having been taken away in his fantasy. The third patient, a middle-aged female with chronic schizophrenia, who gave another such response, by responding to Card VIII, saying "Two seals. They are seals, because their legs and arms are quite short. They look like muscles. Only the muscles of seals. With backbones here." In this response, she saw two aquatic animals that have intrinsically diminished (short) legs and arms, and this image soon became muscles with backbones.

Starting with these findings, the attempts were made further to find similar responses in their Rorschach percepts. It was found that the responses in which a mass of flesh or muscles are explicitly verbalized are not often seen in their Rorschach percepts, but that the responses with the same implications in modified and implicit forms, especially in the form of animals or human beings with diminution of head, legs or arms, were quite common in schizophrenic patients.

Although apparently different, these responses share the common characteristic of revealing the perception of a mass of flesh in the Rorschach pattern. The author called the above percept "a mass of flesh" (MF) and considered that the implications of the MFs should be studied further in the diagnosis of schizophrenia. In order to detect MFs reliably, inclusion and exclusion criteria for MFs were developed which describes the details to identify the MFs.

First, this study is an attempt to develop inclusion criteria for detecting these responses based on these observations. Second, to examine whether perception of MFs is characteristic in schizophrenia or not, the presence or absence of the MFs was examined in the Rorschach protocols of patients in the diagnostic groups of acute schizophrenia, anxiety disorders according to DSM-IV criteria, and healthy adults.

Method

Inclusion and Exclusion Criteria for the MF Percept

The idea that schizophrenics produce percepts of a mass of flesh evolved through our earlier observations in the evaluation of 7 chronic schizophrenia patients. Thereafter, particular attention was given to the responses of 69 consecutive chronic schizophrenic patients (76 in total) to confirm whether or not they produced any response which had a connotation of a mass of flesh or its implicit representation, mainly reflected in diminution of head, arms or legs, of any living thing. After it was confirmed that 75 out of 76 (98%) chronic schizophrenic patients produced some MFs, a list of criteria for MFs was made to detect them reliably.

MFs are, in their explicit and typical form, responses in which a mass of flesh or muscle is explicitly verbalized. The MFs, in their implicit forms, include responses in which diminution of arm, leg, and head is mentioned. In these responses, absence, unusual shortness or vagueness of arms, legs or head is verbalized. The things or living things with a mass-like shape, or perceived as folded or unfolded, are also included because these responses reflect the image of a mass of flesh or the process of becoming a mass of flesh or its denial. Exclusion criteria were made as a guide to exclude misleading responses. Inclusion and exclusion criteria are summarized in Appendix 2.

Test Administration and Scoring

All Rorschach tests were administered by the present authors. The presence or absence of any response that fit the criteria was examined in each case. The cases were divided into two groups, that is, one with MFs and one without.

Inter-Rater Reliability

Inter-rater agreement was determined by evaluating the MFs according to the protocols of 20 chronic schizophrenics. Independent ratings was made by two raters. Nineteen among 20 protocols were scored as showing MF (MF +) by two independent scorers, and 95% inter-rater agreement was obtained.

Subjects

The socio-demographic data of the subjects used for evaluation of the MFs are shown in Table 13. The chronic schizophrenic patients were those of Study 2, who agreed to participate to the study using the Rorschach test. There were 41 men and 35 women. The mean (SD) age of the patients was 49.4 (9.4) years. The mean (SD) chlorpromazine-equivalent dose was 474.8 (406.3) mg. Twenty-two acute schizophrenic patients, 10 male and 12 female, are inpatients of a hospital in a Tokyo suburb. The Rorschach test was administered within one month after their first admission. Their mean (SD) age was 21.8 (3.3) years. All of them were medicated, and the mean (SD) chlorpromazine-equivalent dose was 1082.3 (536.8) mg. All of them had been diagnosed with schizophrenia, according to DSM-IV criteria. Thirty patients with anxiety disorders according to DSM-IV, 16 male and 14 female, were outpatients of a private clinic in Tokyo. Their mean (SD) age was 35.9 (13.4) years. Twenty-eight healthy adults, 14 men and 14 women, were graduate students, hospital staff members, businessmen, office employees, and housewives. The mean (SD) age was 34.1 (12.8) years old. All normal adults were demonstrated to be healthy by administering General Health Questionnaire (Goldberg, 1972; Goldberg and Williams, 1988). Written informed consent was also obtained. (See Table 13.)

Table 13. Demographic characteristics of subjects. (Study 5.)

	Schizophrenia		Anxiety Disorders	Nprmals
	Chronic	Acute		
	(N=76)	(N=22)	(N=30)	(N=22)
Mean Age	49.4	21.8	35.9	34.1
Gender (% male)	53.9	45.5	53.3	50.0

Statistics

The number of subjects perceiving MFs and those not perceiving MF was calculated in each diagnostic group.

Results

Seventy-five out of 76 chronic schizophrenic patients (98%) saw MFs. All 22 acute schizophrenic patients saw MFs. Twenty-eight out of 30 patients with anxiety disorders did not perceive MF. None of the healthy adults saw the MF. It would be reasonable to regard the MFs as characteristic of schizophrenia. The number of subjects perceiving MFs (MF+) and those not perceiving MF (MF-) in schizophrenic and non-schizophrenic groups are shown in Table 14 (x^2 = 11.308, df=1, p=0.001).

Table 14. MFs in schizophrenic and non-schizophrenic groups. (Study 5)

	Schizophrenic		Non-schizophrenic	
	Acute	Chronic	Anxiety Disorders	Normal
	(N=22)	(N=76)	(N=30)	(N=28)
MF+	22	75	2	0
MF-	0	1	28	28

Both of two patients with anxiety disorders who perceived MFs were young adolescent males and had brief psychotic episodes in their life histories. One patient with chronic schizophrenia who did not perceive MF was a middle-aged male patient who scored the least total response to the inkblots. (His total response was less than ten.)

Discussion

The primary contribution of this investigation is to find that Rorschach percepts of a mass of flesh are characteristic of schizophrenia. It was found that although there are some differences in their responses, the perception of a mass of flesh in Rorschach inkblot stimuli was broadly seen as living things with diminished arms, legs or head. By developing inclusion and exclusion criteria for MFs, detection of MFs would become easier and more reliable. To test whether the perception of MFs in inkblots is unique to schizophrenia or not, we examined the Rorschach Test data of 22 acute schizophrenia, 30 anxiety disorders and 28 healthy adults. Ninety-seven out of 98 schizophrenic patients saw MFs, although only two out of 30 patients with anxiety disorders saw MFs. Further, healthy adults did not see any MF. Thus, MFs proved to be characteristic of schizophrenia.

An index for detecting such responses is particularly important because it provides a tool for detecting schizophrenia in its early phase. Ninety-eight percent of chronic schizophrenics, as well as 100% of acute schizophrenic patients, perceived MFs. The perception of MFs might exist from the time of onset and therefore be able to detect a very early phase of schizophrenia, suggesting the diagnostic predictive value of MF perception. As a greater understanding of the nature of schizophrenia has refocused attention on the early course of psychosis in the from of early detection and intervention around the onset (McGlashan and Johannessen, 1996) the inclusion and exclusion criteria would have more value if MFs are found in the prodrome of schizophrenia.

The findings that schizophrenic patients produce MF percepts may lead to improvement of our understanding of thought disorder of schizophrenia. The use of the Rorschach test in the study of thought disorder is well established. However, using the Rorschach test for the purpose of eliciting perceptual deficits, manifested in global and affective percepts such as MFs, might provide a new opportunity to understand the cognitive dysfunction of schizophrenia patients.

Conclusion

The Rorschach test was given to schizophrenic and non-schizophrenic subjects to determine whether schizophrenic patients more frequently produced the “mass of flesh” percept than the non-schizophrenic groups did.

Chapter 4

Discussion and Conclusion

Discussion

The major findings of the studies on schizophrenics' body image aberration in this chapter are: (1) There is some aberration in schizophrenics' body image. (2) There are aberrant as well as intact phases in their body images. (3) Aberration was found in functional imageries, while anatomical imageries are intact. (4) Aberration is independent of symptoms and conventional neuroleptic medication.

The main questions raised in the introduction were whether aberration comes from symptoms or is an effect of neuroleptics, and whether it is remediable or not. What the components of body image are and which phase of body image is aberrant in schizophrenia was the first question we tried to answer by attempts at classification of body image items by factor analysis. Nine body image factors were obtained, and some factors proved to differentiate schizophrenics from normal controls. Although these factors were variously named, after rather exhaustive attempts, the only discrete common feature among factor-analytic studies was that functional imageries may contribute substantially to the factors that meaningfully differentiated groups or were related to depression. In addition, almost no significant correlation was found between aberrant body image factors and clinical characteristics such as symptoms, insight, or neuroleptic dosage. The results of Study 1 showed that when each component of symptoms and insight was cross-validated to the BIQ factors, there were some symptoms and some insight components related to body image factors; however, the overall results showed their relationship was quite weak. The only strong evidence gained through these studies was the fact that there are some differential body image factors, most of which seemed to relate to functional body imageries, but none of which seemed to relate to the anatomical component of body image of schizophrenia.

Thus the question of which phase of body image links with symptoms and which to recovery? leads to the next question, "What are the body images of schizophrenics and what is aberrant for them?" In Study 2, attempts were made to clarify this question simply by comparing three hypothetical components of body image, that is, anatomical, functional, and psychological, between schizophrenic and non-schizophrenic groups. The results showed clearly that anatomical, that is, the visual or the spatial, component is intact in schizophrenia and limited their aberration mainly to functional component.

The fact that schizophrenics have aberrant body images in function, i.e., they have unmovable body images, is controversial with regard to the possibility that it reflects perseverance in motor activity. Schizophrenic patients might have difficulty in the shifting the response set in motor activity in light of the feedback that a previous response was incorrect and consequently "persevere" in making the same response, creating difficulty in movement cognition. Perseveration is a cardinal feature of frontal lobe disease (Bilder and Goldberg, 1987). It is one of the presenting basic neurocognitive deficits, observed since the time of Bleuler (1911/1950), who wrote that schizophrenic patients "remain fixed to the same circle of ideas, the same words, the same sentence structure or at any rate, return to them again and again without any logical need."

The degree of perseverance of schizophrenic patients is similar to that of patients with known frontal pathology (Levin, 1984). Since Weinberger et al. (1986) reported a negative correlation between the percentage perseveration as measured by the Wisconsin Card Sorting Test, WCST, (Milner, 1963) and prefrontal blood flow, these associations have supported the hypothesis that schizophrenic patients have an impairment of the frontal or prefrontal cortex.

Because the clinical interpretation of test data can often point to multiple studies that converge on a set of frequent severe and selective deficits, patients with schizophrenia typically demonstrate abnormalities in attention, memory, and executive function that stand out against a background of diffuse impairment (Pantelis et al., 1996). However, some areas of function appear to be relatively more intact than others, i.e., some aspects of language (Gold et al., 1994; Saykin et al., 1991; Daniels et al., 1988; Barr et al., 1989; Frith, 1993) and some types of visual spatial processing (Kolb and Whishaw, 1983; Goldberg et al., 1990; Goldberg et al., 1993a). These neuropsychological profiles implicate specific brain regions, i.e., frontal-medial dysfunction (Kolb and Whishaw, 1983; Taylor and Abrams, 1984). The finding that the aberration referred to functional body imageries would imply body image deficits that have some relation to dorsolateral deficits, and the fact that the anatomical, that is, visual and spatial, imageries remain intact is consistent with the previous finding that some types of visual spatial processing is intact in the neuropsychological profile of schizophrenics.

In Study 3, body image aberration was considered through an attempt to detect specific body image characteristics related to depression in schizophrenia by comparing the BIQ factor scores between depressive and non-depressive groups comprised by Zung's Self-rating Depression Scale (SDS) in normal and schizophrenic groups respectively. The results showed some body image factors related uniquely to depression in schizophrenia, which, again, referred to functional body images. The result of this part of the study might cast light on future prospects of the study of body image aberration using a device such as the BIQ because of its link with DSS which has become a target for treatment of schizophrenia, with the novel antipsychotic medications. The studies performed for this chapter all revealed that neuroleptics did not relate to body image aberration; however, novel antipsychotic agents were not discussed or studied. This would be relevant to the final question as to whether or not the body image aberration is remediable.

Study 4 and Study 5 are reports of subsidiary findings of our main studies using the BIQ, in which schizophrenic patients produced Rorschach responses implying or referring to "mass of flesh." Study 4 is composed of the initial observations. In Study 5, the Rorschach test was given to schizophrenic and non-schizophrenic subjects to determine whether schizophrenic patients more frequently produced the "mass of flesh" percept than the non-schizophrenic groups did. These findings suggest that there might be a fear of immobility in schizophrenia that is congruent with our main findings.

CONCLUSION

Schizophrenic body image aberration was considered in the current context. The schizophrenic body image aberration was unrelated to symptoms, insight, or conventional neuroleptic medication, but proved to be germane to schizophrenia. The schizophrenic body image aberration also proved to be limited to functional imagery while anatomical imageries remained intact.

ACKNOWLEDGEMENTS

We would like to express our appreciation to Dr. Chin-Piao Chien, professor emeritus of UCLA, and Dr. Shoji Shin'ichi and Dr. Susumu Oda, professors emeriti of Tsukuba University. We also thank Dr. Toshihiko Maeda of tne Institute of Statistical Mathematics for the statistical consultation.

Part of the text was re-edited from *Psychiatry and Clinical Neurosciences,* Vol. 56, pp9-15, "Body image, symptoms and insight in chronic schizophrenia" by Koide et al (2002), with permission from Blackwell Publishing, and from *Comprehensive Psychiatry,* Vol.43, pp474-477, "A mass of flesh: Schizophrenic Rorschach Percepts" by Koide R., et al (2002), with permission from Elsevier.

APPENDIX

Appendix 1. Manual for Scoring the Body Image Questionnaire

Appendix 1-1. Overview of the Questionnaire and the Scoring System

Reverse items The BIQ is composed of 59 items, including 28 reverse questions. Reverse items are Nos. 2, 4, 7, 12, 13, 14, 15, 22, 26, 27, 28, 30, 31, 33, 35, 36, 37, 38, 42, 43, 44, 46, 48, 50, 52, 55, 57 and 59.

Scoring system In *Regular items*, answers are scored as 7 when one "strongly agrees" with the statements, and scored as 1 when one "strongly disagrees" to the statements. In the *Reverse items*, answers are scored as 1 when one "strongly agrees" with the statements, and scored as 7 when one "strongly disagrees" with the statements. Answers as "neither agree nor disagree" are scored as 4.

BIQ component BIQ has three Components, Anatomical, Functional and Psychological. *Anatomical items* are Nos. 4, 8, 15, 16, 18, 20, 24, 28, 36, 40, 44, 48, 52, 54, 55, 56, 57 and 58. (See Apendix 1-3.) *Functional items* are: Nos. 1, 2, 3, 5, 9, 13, 17, 21, 25, 33, 37, 38, 41, 42, 47 and 53. (See Appendix 1-4.) *Psychological items* are Nos. 6, 7, 10, 11, 12, 14, 19, 22, 23, 26, 27, 29, 30, 31, 32, 34, 35, 39, 43, 45, 46, 49, 50, 51 and 59. (See Appendix 1-5.)

Appendix 1-2. Body Image Questionnaire (BIQ)

	Strongly disagree						
		Moderately disagree					
			Slightly agree				
				Neither agree nor disagree			
					Slightly agree		
						Moderately agree	
							Strongly agree
01. My body is weak.							
02. My eyesight is good. ®							
03. I often get sick.							
04. My complexion is pale. ®							
05. My body is limber.							
06. My body is underdeveloped.							
07. My body is clean.®							
08. I am short.							
09. I move slowly							
10. My body is defective.							
11. My body feels cold.							
12. My body is beautiful.®							
13. I am good at athletics.®							
14. I am becoming stronger. ®							
15. My body is skinny. ®							
16. My body is small.							
17. I often lose my balance.							
18. I have small eyes.							
19. I am often injured.							
20. I am poorly proportioned.							
21. I walk slowly.							
22. I seldom feel tired.®							
23. My mood is numb.							
24. My body is rough.							
25. I am clumsy with my hands.							
26. I seldom catch a cold.®							
27. I am satisfied with my body. ®							
28. I am thin.®							
29. My voice is feeble.							
30. My skin is not easily poisoned. ®							
31. I am always cheerful. ®							
32. My body is unattractive.							

Appendix 1-2 (Continued)

33. My posture is good. ®							
34. I always feel sick.							
35. I am not allergic to many things. ®							
36. My skin is smooth.®							
37. I can work well in dark rooms. ®							
38. My stomach is not unusually strong. ®							
39. My body is susceptible to infection.							
40. My hands are not unusually large.							
4I. I cannot move my body freely.							
42. My heart is strong. ®							
43. I don't mind being touched by others. ®							
44. My body is not meager.®							
45. I seldom get excited.							
46. My health is getting better. ®							
47. My teeth are weak.							
48. My body is symmetrical.®							
49. I am seldom tense.							
50. I am not prone to bump into others. ®							
51. My body is not consistent with my sex.							
52. My body is rectangular. ®							
53. My bowels are unusually strong.							
54. My legs are unusually short.							
55. My arms are unusually long. ®							
56. My neck is unusually long.							
57. My head is large. ®							
58. My hair is unusually short.							
59. I always feel energetic.®							

®=reverse item.

Appendix 1-3. BIQ-Anatomical items

04. My complexion is pale. ®
08. I am short.
15. My body is skinny. ®
16. My body is small.
18. I have small eyes.
20. I am poorly proportioned.
24. My body is rough.
28. I am thin. ®
36. My skin is smooth. ®
40. My hands are not unusually large.

Appendix 1-3. (Continued)

44. My body is not meager. ®.
48. My body is symmetrical. ®.
52. My body is rectangular. ®
54. My legs are unusually short.
55. My arms are unusually long. ®
56. My neck is unusually long.
57. My head is large. ®
58. My hair is unusually short.

®=reverse item.

Appendix 1-4. BIQ-Functional items

01. My body is weak.
02. My eyesight is good. ®
03. I often get sick.
05. My body is limber.
09. I move slowly
13. I am good at athletics.®
17. I often lose my balance.
21. I walk slowly.
25. I am clumsy with my hands.
33. My posture is good. ®
37. I can work well in dark rooms. ®
38. My stomach is not unusually strong. ®
41. I cannot move my body freely.
42. My heart is strong. ®
47. My teeth are weak.
53. My bowels are unusually strong.

®=reverse item.

Appendix 1-5. BIQ Psychological items

06. My body is underdeveloped.
07. My body is clean. ®
10. My body is defective.
11. My body feels cold.
12. My body is beautiful. ®
14. I am becoming stronger. ®
19. I am often injured.
22. I seldom feel tired. ®

Appendix 1-5. (Continued)

23. My mood is numb.
26. I seldom catch a cold. ®
27. I am satisfied with my body. ®
29. My voice is feeble.
30. My skin is not easily poisoned. ®
31. I am always cheerful. ®
32. My body is unattractive.
34. I always feel sick.
35. I am not allergic to many things. ®
39. My body is susceptible to infection.
43. I don't mind being touched by others. ®
45. I seldom get excited.
46. My health is getting better. ®
49. I am seldom tense.
50. I am not prone to bump into others. ®
51. My body is not consistent with my sex.
59. I always feel energetic.®

Appendix 2. Inclusion and exclusion criteria for perception of flesh masses

Inclusion
1. Explicit verbalization of a mass of flesh or muscles.
2. The remains of a mass of flesh.
3. Diminution of head, arm or leg.
4. Elongation of neck, arm or leg.
5. Plants or vehicles described as "without arms or legs.[1]"
6. A creature with the shape of a mass[2].
7. A single organ vaguely detected with no further explanation.
8. "Being cut and opened," "being folded," "being unfolded," or "being stuck together".
Exclusion
1. Underdeveloped animals or human beings, or animals that have intrinsically short arms or legs, without further explanation concerning diminution of arms or legs.
2. Omission of legs in the response to Card VII.

Note: 1. Examples are: "A tropical flower. I cannot find its arms or legs." "An airplane. It doesn't have any arms or legs." 2. Example is: "A prawn. It is in this globular shape, with his back hunching up in this way."

References

Amador, X. F., Flaum, M,, Andreasen, N.C., Strauss, D. H., Yale, S. A., Clark, S. C. and Gorman, J. M. (1994). Awareness of illness in schizophrenia and schizoaffective and Mood disorders. *Archives of General Psychiatry, 51*, 826-836.

Amador, X. F., Strauss, D.H., Yale, S.A., and Gorman JM. (1991). Awareness of illness in schizophrenia. *Schizophrenia Bulletin, 17*,113-132.

American Psychiatric Association. (1980). *Diagnostic and statistical manual of mental disorders (3rd edition)*. Washington, DC: American Psychiatric Association.

American Psychiatric Association. (1987). *Diagnostic and statistical manual of mental disorders (3rd edition revised)*. Washington, DC: American Psychiatric Association.

American Psychiatric Association. (1994). *Diagnostic and statistical manual of mental disorders (4th edition)*. Washington, DC: American Psychiatric Association.

Andreasen, N. C. (1981). *Scale for the assessment of negative symptoms*. Iowa City, IA: The University of Iowa Press.

Andreasen, N. C. (1983). *Scale for the assessment of positive symptoms*. Iowa City, IA: The University of Iowa Press.

Andreasen, N. C., Arndt, S., Alliger, R., Miller, D., and Flaum, M. (1995). Symptoms of schizophrenia: methods, meanings, and mechanisms. *Archives of General Psychiatry, 52*, 341-351.

Andreasen, N, and Bardach, J. (1977). Dysmorphophobia:Symptom or disease? *American Journal of Psychiatry, 134*, 673-676.

Angyal, A. (1936). Experiences of body self in schizophrenia. *Archives of Neurology and Psychiatry, 35*, 1629-1634.

Apter, J.T. (1981). The "silent" acute abdomen in schizophrenia. *Journal of the Medical Society of New Jersey, 78*, 679-680.

Arieti, S. (1945). Primitive habits and perceptual alterations in the terminal stage of schizophrenia. *Archives of Neurology and Psychiatry, 53*, 378-384.

Barr, W. B., Bilder, R. M., Goldberg, E. H., Caplan, E., and Mukherjee, S. (1989). The neuropsychology of schizophrenic speech. *Journal of Communication Disorders, 22*, 327-349.

Berman, A. L. (1972). Videotape self-confrontation of schizophrenic ego and thought processes. *Journal of Consulting and Clinical Psychology, 39,* 78-85.

Bickerstaff, L. K., Harris, S. C, Leggett R S, and Cheah K. C. (1988). Pain insensitivity in schizophrenic patients: A surgical dilemma. *Archives of Surgery, 123*, 49-50.

Bilder, R. M., and Goldberg, R. E. (1987) Motor perseverations in schizoiphrenia. *Archives of Clinical Neuropsychology, 2*, 195-214.

Birtchnell, S. A. (1988). Dysmorphophobia - a centenary discussion. *British Journal of Psychiatry, 153 (suppl 2)*, 41-43.

Blackmore, S. (1986). Out-of-body experiences in schizophrenia. A questionnaire survey. *Journal of Nervous and Mental Disease, 174*, 615-619.

Bleuler, E. (1911) *Dementia Praecox, or the Group of Schizophrenias*. Translated by J Zinkin. New York: International Universities Press (1950).

Braff, D. L., Heaton, R., Kuck, J., Cullum, M., Moranville, J., Grant, I., and Zisook, S. (1991). The generalized pattern of neuropsychological deficits in outpatients with chronic schizophrenia with heterogeneous Wisconsin Card Sorting Test results. *Archives of General Psychiatry, 158*, 340-345.

Brebion, G., Smith, M. J., Amador, X., Malaspina, D., and Gorman, J.M. (1997). Clinical correlates of memory in schizophrenia: differential links between depression, positive and negative symptoms, and two types of memory impairment. *American Journal of Psychiatry, 154*, 1538-1543.

Bryson, G., Bell, M., Lysaker, P. (1997). Affect recognition in schizophrenia: A function of global impairment or a specific cognitive deficit. *Psychiatry Research, 71*, 105-113.

Buchanan, R. W., Strauss, M. E., Breier, A., Kirkpatrick, B., and Carpenter, W.T. (1997). Attentional impairements in deficit and nondeficit forms of schizophrenia. *American Journal of Psychiatry, 154*, 363-370.

Burgess, J. W. (1991). Relationship of depression and cognitive impairment to self-injury in borderline personality disorder, major depression, and schizophrenia. *Psychiatry Research, 38*, 77-87.

Bychowsky, G. (1943). Disorders of the body image in the clinical picture of psychoses. *Journal of Nerveous and Mental Disease, 97*, 310-334.

Caldwell, C. B., and Gottesman, I.I. (1990). Schizophrenics kill themselves too: a review of risk factors for suicide. *Schizophrenia Bulletin, 16*, 571-589.

Cancro, R. (1971). Sophistication of body concept in process-reactive schizophrenia. *Perceptual and Motor Skills, 32*, 567-570.

Cassens, G., Inglis, A. K., Appelbaum, P. S., and Gutheil, T. G. (1990). Neuroleptics: Effects on neuropsychological function in chronic schizophrenic patients. *Schizophrenia Bulletin, 16*, 477-499.

Censits, D. M., Ragland, J. D., Gur, R. C., and Gur, R. E. (1997). Neuropsychological evidence supporting a neurodevelopmental model of schizophrenia: A longitudinal study. *Schizophrenia Research, 24*, 289-298.

Chapman, L. J., Chapman, J.P., and Raulin, M. L. (1976). Scales for physical and social anhedonia. *Journal of Abnormal Psychology, 85*, 374-382.

Chapman, L. J., Chapman, J. P., and Raulin, M. L. (1978). Body-image aberration in schizophrenia. *Journal of Abnormal Psychology, 87*, 399-407.

Cleveland, S. E. (1960a). Body image changes associated with personality reorganization. *Journal of Consulting Psychology, 24*, 256-261.

Cleveland, S. E. (1960b). Judgements of body size in a schizophrenic and a control group. *Psychological Reports, 7*, 304.

Cleveland, S. E., Fisher, S., Reitman, E. E., and Rothaus, P. (1962). Perception of body size in schizophrenia. *Archives of General Psychiatry, 7*, 277-285.

Cohen, L. J., Test, M. A. and Brocon, R. L. (1990). Suicide and schizophrenia: data from a prospective community treatment study. *American Journal of Psychiatry, 147*, 602-607. Correction, 147, 1110.

Coleman, M. J., Carpenter, J. T., Waterneaux, C., Levy, D. L., Shenton, M. E., Perry, J., Medoff, D., Wong, H., Manoach, D., Meyer, P., O'Brien, C., Valentino, C., Robinson, D., Smith, M., Makowski, D. and Holzman, P. S. (1993) The Thought Disorder Index: A reliability study. *Psychological Assessment, 5*, 336-342.

Coleman, M. J., Levy, D. L., Lenzenweger, M. F. and Holzman, P. S. (1996) Thought disorder, perceptual aberrations, and schizotypy. *Journal of Abnormal Psychology, 105*, 469-473.

Connolly, F. and Gipson, M. (1978). Dysmorphophobia. A long term study. *British Journal of Psychiatry, 132*, 458-470.

Coons, P. M., Ascher-Svanum, H, and Bellis, K. (1986). Self-amputation of the female breast. *Psychosomatics, 27*, 667-668.

Cornblatt, B. A., Lenzenweger, M. F., Dworkin, R. H. and Erlenmeyer-Kimling, L. (1985). Positive and negative schizophrenic symptoms, attention, and information processing. *Schizophrenia Bulletin, 11*, 397-408.

Crider, A. (1997). Perseverations in schiziophrenia. *Schizophrenia Bulletin, 23*, 63-74.

Crow, T. J. and Johnstone, E. C. (1980). Dementia praecox and schizophrenia: was Bleuler wrong? *Journal of the Royal College of Physicians, 14*, 238-240.

Crow, T. J. and Stevens, M. (1978). Age disorientation in chronic schizophrenia: the nature of the cognitive deficit. *British Journal of Psychiatry, 133*, 137-142.

Cuesta, M. J. and Peralta, V. (1994). Lack of insight in schizophrenia. *Schizophrenia Bulletin, 20*, 359-366.

Cuesta, M. S., Peralta, V., Caro, F, and de Leon, J. (1995). Schizophrenia syndrome and Wisconsin Card Sorting Test dimensions. *Psychiatry Research, 58*, 45-51.

Daniels, E. K., Shenton, M. E., Holzman, P. S., Benowitz, L. I., Coleman, M. ,Levin, S. and Levine, D. (1988). Patterns of thought disorder associated with right cortical damage, schizophrenia, and mania. *American Journal of Psychiatry, 145*, 944-949.

Darby, J. A. (1968). Pychotheraputic treatment of schizophrenia: Theory and case study. *Psychotherapy: Theory, Research, and Practice, 5*, 234-239.

David, S. A. (1990). Insight and psychosis. *British Journal of Psychiatry, 156*, 798-808.

Delaplaine, R., Ifabumuyi, O. I., Merskey, H. and Zarfas, J. (1978). Significance of pain in psychiatirc hospital patients. *Pain, 4*, 361-366.

deLeon, J., Bott, A. and Simpson, G. H. (1989). Dysmorphophobia: body dysmorphic disorder or delusional disorder, somatic type? *Comprehensive Psychiatry, 30*, 457-472.

Des Lauriers, A. M. (1962). *The experience of reality in childhood schizophrenia.* New York: International Universities Press.

Dillon, D. J. (1962) Measurement of perceived body size. *Perceptual and Motor Skills,14*, 191-196.

Dingman, C. W. and McGlashan, T. H. (1986). Discriminating characteristics of suicides: Chestnut Lodge follow-up sample including patients with affective disorder, schizophrenia and schizoaffective disorder. *Acta Psychiatrica Scandinavica, 74*, 91-97.

Dingman, C. W. and McGlaschan, T. H. (1988). Characteristics of patients with serious suicidal inpatients who ultimately commit suicide. *Hospital and Community Psychiatry, 39*, 295-299.

Di-Nuovo, S., Laicardi, C. and Tobino, C. (1988). Rorschach indices for discriminating between two schizophrenic syndromes. *Perceptual and Motor Skills, 67*, 399-406.

Drake, R. E. and Cotton, P. G. (1986). Depression, hopelessness and suicide in chronic schizophrenia. *British Journal of Psychiatry, 148*, 554-559.

Dworkin, R. H. (1994). Pain insensitivity in schizophrenia: A neglected phenomenon and some implications. *Schizophrenia Bulletin, 20*, 235-248.

Dworkin, R. H. and Caligor, E. (1988). Psychiatric diagnosis and chronic pain: DSM III-R and beyond. *Journal of Pain and Symptom Management, 3*, 87-98.

Edgerton, M., Jacobsen, W. and Meyer, E. (1960) Surgical/ psychiatric study of patients seeking plastic (cosmetic) surgery: 98 consecutive patients with minimal deformity. *British Journal of Plastic Surgery, 13*, 136-145.

Exner, E. J. Jr. (1974). *The Rorschach: A Comprehensive System: Vol.1.* Basic Foundations. New York: Wiley.

Exner, E. J. Jr. (1978). *The Rorschach: A Comprehensive System: Vol.2.* Current Research and Advanced Interpretation. New York: Wiley.

Exner, E. J. Jr. (1986a). *The Rorschach: A Comprehensive System: Vol.1.* Basic Foundations. 2nd ed. New York: Wiley.

Exner, E. J. Jr. (1986b). Some Rorschach data comparing schizophrenics with borderline and schizotypal personality disorders. *Journal of Personality Assessment, 50*, 455-471.

Exner, E. J. Jr. (1991). *The Rorschach: A Comprehensive System: Vol.2.* Current Research and Advanced Interpretation. 2nd ed. New York: Wiley.

Exner EJ Jr. (1993). *The Rorschach: A Comprehensive System: Vol.1.* Basic Foundations (3rd edition). New York: Wiley.

Federn P. (1952). *Ego Psychology and the psychosis.* New York: Basic Books.

Feldman MD. 1988 The challenge of self-mutilation: a review. *Comprehensive Psychiatry, 29*, 252-269.

Ferenczi, S. (1926). The problem of acceptance of unpleasant ideas: Advances in knowledge of the sense of reality. *International Journal of Psychoanalysis, 7*, 312-323.

Fishbain, D. A. (1982) Pain insensitivity in psychosis. *Annals of Emergency Medicine, 11*, 630-632.

Fisher, S. (1963). A further appraisal of the body boundary concept. *Journal of Consulting Psychology, 27*, 62-74.

Fisher, S. (1964). Body image and psychopathology. *Archives of General Psychiatry, 10*, 519-529.

Fisher, S. (1966). Body image in neurotic and schizophrenic patients. *Archives of General Psychiatry, 15*, 90-101.

Fisher, S. and Cleveland, S. E. (1958). *Body image and personality.* Princeton, NJ; Van Nostrand.

Fisher, S. and Cleveland S. E. (1968). *Body image and personality 2nd edition).* New York: Dover Publications.

Fisher, S. and Renik, O.D. (1966). Induction of body image boundary changes. *Journal of Projective Techniques and Personality Assessment, 30*, 429-434.

Fisher, S. and Seidner, R. (1963). Body experiences of schizophrenic, neurotic and normal women. *Journal of Nervous and Mental Disease, 137*, 252-257.

Fottrell, E. (1980). A study of violent behaviour among patients in psychiatric hospitals. *British Journal of Psychiatry, 136*, 216-221.

Freeman, T., Cameron, J. L. and McGhie, A. (1958). *Chronic Schizophrenia.* New York: International Universities Press.

Freeman, T. and Gathercole, L. E. (1966). Perseveration in chronic schizophrenia and organic dementia. *British Journal of Psychiatry, 112*, 27-32.

Freud, S. (1962). *The ego and the id.* New York: Norton.

Frith, C. (1993). *The Cognitive Neuropsychology of Schizophrenia.* Erlbaum, Hove.

Galdi, J. (1983). The causality of depression in schizophrenia. *British Journal of Psychiatry, 142*, 621-624.

George, L. and Neufeld, R. W. (1985). Cognition and symptomatology in schizophrenia. *Schizophrenia Bulletin, 11*, 264-285.

Gerstmann, J. (1942). Problem of imperception of disease and of impaired body territories with organic lesions. Relation to body schema and its disorders. *Archives of Neurology and Psychiatry, 48*, 890-913.

Gold, J. M., Hermann, B.P., Wyler, A., Randolph, C., Goldberg, T.E. and Weinberger, D. R. (1994). Schizophrenia and temporal lobe epilepsy: a neuropsychological study. *Archives of General Psychiatry, 51*, 265-272.

Goldberg, D. P. (1972). *The detection of psychiatric illness by questionnaire.* Maudsley Monograph 21. London: Oxford University Press.

Goldberg, D. and Williams, P. (1988). *A user's guide to the General Health Questionnaire.* Windsor, Berkshire: Neer-Nelson.

Goldberg, T. E., Gold, J. M., Greenberg, R., Griffin, S., Schulz, S. C., Picker, D., Kleinman, J. E., and Weinberger, D. R. (1993a). Contrasts between patients with affective disorder and patients with schizophrenia on a neuropsychological screening test battery. *American Journal of Psychiatry, 150*, 1355-1362.

Goldberg, T. E., Greenberg, R. and Griffin, S. (1993b). The impact of clozapine on cognition and psychiatric symptoms in patients with schizophrenia. *British Journal of Psychiatry, 162*, 43-48.

Goldberg, T.E., Ragland, D.R., Gold, J., Bigelow, L.B., Torrey, E.F. and Weinberger, D. R. (1990). Neuropsychological assessment of monozygotic twins discordant for schizophrenia. *Archives of General Psychiatry 47*, 1066-1072.

Goldstein, G. (1978). Cognitive and perceptual differences between schizophrenics and organics. *Schizophrenia Bulletin, 4*, 160-185.

Goodenough, F. L. (1928). Studies in the psychology of children's drawings. *Psychological Bulletin, 25,* 272-279.

Green, M. F. (1996). What are the functional consequences of neurocognitive deficit in schizophrenia? *American Journal of Psychiatry, 153*, 321-330.

Green, M. F., Marshall, B. D., Wirshing, W. C., Ames, D., Marder, S. R., McGurk, S., Kern, R. S. and Mintz, J. (1997). Does risperidone improve verbal working mempry in treatment–resistant schizophrenia? *American Journal of Psychiatry, 154*, 799-804.

Green, M. F. and Nuechterlein, K. H. (1999). Should schizophrenia be treated as a neurocognitive disorder? *Schizophrenia Bulletin, 25*, 309-318.

Green, M. F., Nuechterlein, K. H. and Geier, D.J. (1992). Sustained and selective attention in schizophrenia. *Progress in Experimental Personaity and Psychopathology Research, 15*, 290-313.

Green, M. F. and Walker, E. (1985). Neuropsychological performance and positive and negative symptoms in schizophrenia. *Journal of Abnormal Psychology, 94*, 460-469.

Guieu, R., Samuelian, J. C. and Coulouvrat, H. (1994). Objective evaluation of pain perception in patients with schizophrenia. *British Journal of Psychiatry, 164*, 253-255.

Hagger, C., Buckley, P., Kenny, J. T., Friedman, L., Ubogy, D. and Meltzer, H. Y. (1993). Improvement in cognitive functions and psychiatric symptoms in treatment –refractory schizopherenic patients receiving clozapine. *Bioliogical Psychiatry, 34*, 702-712.

Harding, C. M., Zubin, J. and Strauss, S. (1992). Chronicity in schizophrenia. *British Journal of Psychiatry, 161 (Suppl 18)*, 27-37.

Hay, G. (1970). Dysmorphophobia. *British Journal of Psychiatry, 116*, 399-406.

Hay, G. (1973). Changes in psychometric test results following cosmetic nasal operations. *British Journal of Psychiatry, 122*, 89-90.

Hay, G. (1983). Paranoia and dysmorphophobia. *British Journal of Psychiatry, 142*, 309-310.

Head, H. (1911). Sensory disturbunce from cerebral lesions. *Brain, 34*, 187-189.

Head, H. (1926). *Aphasia and Kindred Disorders of Speech.* London: Cambridge University Press.

Heaton, R. K., Baade, L. E. and Johnson, K. L. (1978). Neuropsychological test results associated with psychiatric disorders in adults. *Psychological Bulletin, 85*,141-162.

Hill, G. and Silver, G. (1950). Psychodynamics and esthetic motivations for plastic surgery. *Psychosomatic Medicine, 12*, 345-355.

Hilsenroth, M. J., Fowler, J. C. and Padawer, J. R. (1998). The Rorschach Schizophrenia Index (SCZI): an examination of reliability, validity, and diagnostic efficacy. *Journal of Personality Assessment, 70*, 514-534.

Himelhoch, S., Taylor, S. F., Goldman, R. S. and Tandon, R. (1996). Frontal lobes, antipsychotic medication, and schizophrenic symptoms. *Biological Psychiatry, 39*, 227-229.

Hirsch, S. R. (1982). Depression "revealed" in schizophrenia. *British Journal of Psychiatry, 140*, 421-424.

Hollander, E., Cohen, L. T. and Simeon, D. (1993). Body dysmorphic disorder. *Psychiatric Annals, 23*, 359-364.

Holt, R. (1977). A method for assessing primary process manifestations and their controls in Rorschach responses. In M. Rickers-Ovsiankina (Eds), *Rorschach Psychology (2nd edition, pp375-420)*. Huntington, NY: Krieger.

Holtzman, W. H., Gorham, D. R. and Moran, L. J. (1964). A factor-analytic study of schizophrenic thought processes. *Journal of Abnormal and Social Psychology, 69*, 355-364.

Holtzman, W. H., Thorpe, J. S., Swartz, J. D. and Herron, E.W. (1961*). Inkblot perception and personality: Holtzman inkblot technique*. Austin: University of Texas Press.

Hu, W. H., Sun, C. M., Lee, C. T., Peng, S. L., Lin, S. K. and Shen, W. W. (1991). A clinical study of schizophrenic suicides: 42 cases in Taiwan. *Schizophrenia Research, 5,* 43-50.

Huber, G. (1957). Die coenaesthetische Schizophrenie. *Fortschritte der Neurologie und Psychiatrie, 25*, 491-520.

Huber, G. (1971). Die coenaesthetische Schizophrenie als Praegnanztyp schizophrener Erkrankungen. *Acta Psychiatrica Scandinavica, 47*, 349-362.

Humphreys, M. S., Johnstone, E. C., MacMillan, J. F. and Taylor, P. J. (1992). Dangerous behaviour preceding first admission s for schizophrenia. *British Journal of Psychiatry, 161*, 501-505.

Jacobsen, W., Edgerton, M., Meyer, E., Canter, A. and Slaughter, R. (1960). Psychiatric evaluation of male patients seeking cosmetic surgery. *Plastic and Reconstructive Surgery, 16*, 356-372.

Jasker, R. O. and Reed, M. R. (1963). Assessment of body image organization of hospitalizd and non-hopspitalized subjects. *Journal of Projective Techniques, 27*, 185-190.

Jeste, D. V., Lohr, J. B., Eastman, J. H., Rockwell, E. and Caligiuri, M. P. (1998). Adverse neurobiological effects of long term use of neuroleptics: Human and animal studies. *Journal of Psychiatric Research, 32*, 201-214.

Johnston, M, and Holzman, P. (1979). *Assessing Schizophrenic Thinking*. San Francisco: Jossey-Bass.

Johnstone, E. C., Crow, T. J., Frith, C. D., Husband, J. and kreel, L. (1976). Cerebral ventricular size and cognitive impairment in chronic schizophrenia. *Lancet II*, 924-926.

Katz, E., Kluger, Y., Rabinovici, R., Stein, D. and Gimmon, Z. (1990). Acute surgical abdominal disease in chronic svhizohrenic patients: A unique clinical problem. *Israel Journal of Medical Sciences, 26*, 275-277.

Kay, S. R., Fiszbein, A. and Opler, L.A. (1987). The positive and negative syndrome scale (PANSS) for schizophrenia. *Schizophrenia Bulletin, 13*, 261-276.

Keefe, R. S. E., Silva, S. G., Perkins, D. O. and Lieberman, J. A. (1999). The effects of atypical antipsychotic drugs on neurocognitive impairmaent in schizophrenia: A review and meta-analysis. *Schizophrenia Bulletin, 25*, 201-222.

Kennedy, B. L. and Feldmann, T. B. (1994). Self-inflicted eye injuries: case presentation s and a literature review. *Hospital Community Psychiatry, 45*, 470-474.

Kern, R. S., Green, M. F., Marshall, B. D., Wirshing, W. C., McGurk, S. R., Marder, S. R. and Mintz, J. (1999). Risperidone vs haloperidol on secondary memory: Can newer antipsychotic medications aid learning? *Schizophrenia Bulletin, 25*, 223-233.

Knights, A. and Hirsch, S. R. (1981). "Revealed" depression and drug treatment for schizophrenia. *Archives of General Psychiatry, 38*, 806-811.

Koide, R. (1985). Body image differences between schizophrenic and normal female adults. International *Review of Applied Psychology, 34*, 335-347.

Kokonis, N. D. (1972). Body image disturbance in schizophrenia. A study of arms and feet. *Journal of Personality Assessment, 36*, 573-575.

Kolb, B. and Whishaw, .IQ. (1983). Performance of schizophrenic patients on tests sensitive to left or right frontal temporal, and parietal function in neurologic patients. *Journal of Nervous and Mental Disease, 171*, 435-443.

Kraepelin, E. (1919). *Dementia Praecox and Paraphrenia*. Edinburgh, Scotland: E. and S. Livingstone.

Kuechenhoff, J. (1984).Dysmorphophobie. *Nervenarzt, 55*, 122-126.

Kwawer, J. (1980). Primitive interpersonal modes, borderline phenomena and Rorschach content. In J. Kwawer, H. Lerner, P. Lerner and A. Sugarman (Eds). *Borderline Phenomena and Rorschach Test* (pp. 257-274). New York: International University Press.

Lautenbacher, S. and Krieg, J. C. (1994). Pain perception in psychiatric disorders: a review of the literature. *Journal of Psychiatry Research, 28*, 109-122.

Leventhal, D. B., Schuck, J. R., Clemons, J. T. and Cox, M. (1982). Proprioception in schizophrenia. *Journal of Nervous and Mental Disease, 170*, 21-26.

Levin, S. (1984). Frontal lobe dysfunction in schizophrenia II. Impairments of psychological and brain functions. *Journal of Psychiatric Research, 18*, 27-55.

Liddle, P. F. and Morris, D.L. (1991). Schizophrenic syndromes and frontal lobe performance. *British Journal of Psychiatry, 158*, 340-345.

Linn, L. and Goldman, I. (1949). Psyciatric observations concerning rhinoplasty. *Psychosomatic Medicine, 11*, 307-309.

Lukianowicz, N. (1967). Body image disturbances in psychiatric disorders. *British Journal of Psychiatry, 113*, 31-47.

Lysaker, P. and Bell, M. (1994). Insight and cognitive impairment in schizophrenia: Performance on repeated administrations of the Wisconsin Card Sorting Test. *Journal of Nervous and Mental Disease, 182*, 656-660.

Machover, K. (1949). *Personality projection in the drawing of the human figure. Springfield, III.*: Chales C Thomas.

Malec, J. (1978). Neuropsychological assessment of schizophrenia versus brain damage: a review. *Journal of Nervous and Mental Disease, 166*, 507-516.

Manschreck, T. C., Maher, B. A., Hoover, T. M. and Ames D. (1985). Repetition in schizophrenic speech. *Language and Speech, 28*, 327-349.

Marchand, W. E. (1959). Practice of surgery in a neuropsychiatric hospital. *Archives of General Psychiatry, 1*, 123-131.

Martin, R. L., Cloninger, C. R. and Guze, S. B. (1985). Frequency and differetial diagnosis of depressive syndromes in schizophrenia. *Journal of Clinical Psychiatry, 46*, 9-13.

Martin, T. and Gattaz, W. F. (1991). Psychiatric aspects of male genital self-mutilation. *Psychopathology, 24*, 170-178.

Mason, B., Cohen, J. and Exner, J. E. Jr. (1985). Schizophrenic, depressive, and nonpatient personality organizations described by Rorschach factor structures. *Journal of Personality Assessment, 49*, 295-305.

Mayer-Gross, W. (1920). Uber die Stellungsnahme auf abgelaufenen akuten psychose. *Zeitschrift fuer die Gesamte Neurologie Psychiatrie, 60*, 160-212.

McGlaschan, T. H. and Carpenter, W. T. Jr. (1976). An investigation of the post psychotic depressive syndrome. *American Journal of Psychiatry, 133*, 14-19.

McGlashan, T. H. and Johannessen, J. O. (1996). Early detection and intervention with schizophrenia: Rationale. *Schizophrenia Bulletin, 22*, 201-222.

McGlichrist, I. and Cutting, J. (1995). Somatic delusions in schizophrenia and the affective psychoses. *British Journal of Psychiatry, 167*, 350-361.

Meloy, J. (1984). Thought organization and primary process in the patients of schizophrenics. *British Journal of Medical Psychology, 57*, 279-281.

Meltzer, H. Y. and McGurk, S. R. (1999). The effects of clozapine, risperidone, and olanzapine on cognitive function in schizophrenia. *Schizophrenia Bulletin, 25*, 233-255.

Merriam, A. E., Kay, S., Opler, L. A., Kushner, S. F. and van Praag, H. M. (1990). Neurological signs and the positive-negative dimension in schizophrenia. *Biological Psychiatry, 28*, 181-192.

Merskey, H. (1965). The characteristics of persistent pain in psychological illness. *Journal of Psychosomatic Research, 9*, 291-298.

Meyer, E., Jacobsen, W., Edgerton, M. and Canter, A. (1960). Motivational patterns in patients seeking elective plastic surgery (women who seek rhinoplasty). *Psychosomatic Medicine, 22*, 193-199.

Milner, B. (1963). Effect of different brain lesions in card sorting. The role of the frontal lobes. *Archives of Neurology, 9*, 100-110.

Nuechterlein, K. H., Edell, W. S., Norris, M. and Dawson, M. E. (1986). Attentional vulnerability indicators, thought disorder, and negative symptoms. *Schizophrenia Bulletin, 12*, 408-426.

Oosthuizen, P., Lambert, T. and Castle, D. J. (1998). Dysmorphic concern: prevalence and associations with clinical variables. *Australia and New Zealand Journal of Psychiatry, 32*, 129-132.

Overall, J. E. and Gorham, D. R. (1962). Brief Psychiatric Rating Scale (BPRS). *Psychological Reports, 10*, 799-812.

Pantelis, C., Nelson, H. E. and Barnes, T. R. E. (1996). *Schizophrenia: A neuropsychological perspective*. Chichester, West Sussex: John Wiley and Sons.

Pattison, E. M. and Kahan, T. (1983). The deliberate self-harm syndrome. *American Journal of Psychiatry, 140*, 867-872.

Perry, W. and Braff, D. L. (1994). Information processing and thought disorder in schizophrenia. *American Journal of Psychiatry, 151*, 363-367.

Perry, W. and Braff, D. L. (1998). A multimethod approach to assessing perseveration in schizophrenia patients. *Schizophrenia Research, 33*, 69-77.

Perry, W., Geyer, M. A. and Braff, D. L. (1999). Sensorimotor gating and thought disturbance measured in close temporal proximity in schizophrenic patients. *Archives of General Psychiatry, 56*, 277-281.

Perry, W., Viglione, D. and Braff, D. L. (1992). The Ego Impairment Index and schizophrenia: a validation study. *Journal of Personality Assessment, 59*, 165-175.

Phillips, K. A. (1991). Body dysmorphic disorder: The distress of imagined ugliness. American *Journal of Psychiatry, 148*, 1138-1149.

Phillips, K. A. and McElroy, S. L. (1993). Insight, overvalued ideation, and delusional thinking in body dysmorphic disorder: Theoretical and treatment implications. *Journal of Nervous and Mental Disease, 181*, 699-702.

Phillips, K. A. and McElroy, S. L., Keck, P. E., Hudson, J. I. and Pope, H. G. Jr. (1994). A comparison of delusional and nondelusional body dysmorphic disorder in 100 cases. *Psychopharmacology Bulletin, 30*, 179-186.

Philips, C. and Hunter, M. (1982). Headache in a psychiatric population. *Journal of Nervous and Mental Disease, 170,* 34-40.

Pick, A. (1922). Stoerung der Orientierung am eigenen Koerper. *Psychologische Forschung, 1*, 303-315

Pickar, D. (1995). Prospects for pharmacotherapy of schizophrenia. *Lancet, 345(8949)*, 557-562.

Quinlan, D. M. and Harrow, M. (1974). Boundary disturbance in schizophrenia. *Journal of Abnormal Psychology, 83*, 533-541.

Rado, S. (1959). Dynamics and classification of disorder behavior. *American Journal of Psychiatry, 1*, 651-656.

Reitman, E. E. and Cleveland, S. E. (1964). Changes in body image following sensory deprivation in schizophrenic and control groups. *Journal of Abnormal and Social Psychology, 68*, 168-176.

Renik, O. D. and Fisher, S. (1968). Induction of body image boundary changes in male subjects. *Journal of Projective Techniques and Personality Assessment, 32*, 45-49.

Ritzler, B. and Rosenbaum, G. (1974). Proprioception in schizophrenics and normals: Effects of stimulus intensity and interstimulus interval. *Journal of Abnormal Psychology, 83*, 106-111.

Ritzler, B. (1977). Proprioception and schizophrenia: A replication study with nonschizophrenic patient controls. *Journal of Abnormal Psychology, 86*, 501-504.

Roehricht, F. and Priebe, S. (1996). Body image of patients with acute paranoid schizophrenia: A follow-up study. (Das Koerpererleben von Patienten mit einer akuten paranoiden Schizophrenie. Eine Verlaufsstudie.) *Nervenarzt, 67*, 602-607.

Roehricht, F. and Priebe, S. (1997). Disturbances of body experience in schizophrenic patients.(Stoerungen des Koerpererlebens bei schizophrenen Patienten.) *Fortschritte der Neurologie-Psychiatrie, 65*, 323-336.

Rosenbaum, G., Flenning, F. and Rosen, H. (1965). Effects of weight intensity on discrimination thresholds of normals and schizophrenics. *Journal of Abnormal Psychology,* 70, 446-450.

Rosenthal, S. H., Porter, K. A. and Coffey, B. (1990). Pain insensitivity in schizophrenia: Case report and review of the literature. *General Hospital Psychiatry, 12*, 319-322.

Roy, A., Thompson, R. and Kennedy, S. (1983). Depression in chronic schizophrenia. *British Journal of Psychiatry, 142*, 465-470.

Sacks, M. H., Carpenter, W. T. and Strauss, J. S. (1974). Recovery from delusions. *Archives of General Psychiatry, 30*, 117-120.

Saykin, J. A., Gur, R. C., Gur, R. E., Mozley, P. D., Mozley, L. H., Resnick, S. M, Kester, D. B. and Stafiniak, P. (1991). Neuropsychological function in schizophrenia: selective impairment in memory and learning. *Archives of General Psychiatry, 48*, 618-624.

Schafer, R. (1960). Bodies in Schizophrenic Rorschach Responses. *Journal of Projective Techniques, 24*, 267-281.

Schafer, R. (1986). *Projective Testing and Psychoanalysis. Selected Papers.* International Universities Press, INC.

Scheftel, S., Nathan, A. S., Razin, A. M. and Mezan, P. (1986). A case of radical facial self-mutilation: An unprecedented event and its impact. *Bulletin of the Menninger Clinic, 50*, 525-540.

Schilder, P. (1935). *The image and appearance of the human body*. London: Kegan Paul, Trench, Trubner and Co.

Schmoll, D. (1994). Coenaesthetische Schizophrenie. *Fortschritte der Neurologie Psychiatrie, 62*, 372-378.

Schmoll, D. and Koch, T. (1989). Leibgefuehlsstoerungen in der schizophrenen Psychose. Eine Kasuistik. *Nervenarzt, 60*, 619-627.

Schneider, F., Gur, R. C., Gur, R. E., Shtasel, D. L. (1995). Emotional processing in schizophrenia: Neurobehavioral probes in relation to psychopathology. *Schizophrenia Research, 17*, 67-75.

Schneider, K. (1959). *Klinische Psychopathologie, 12th ed.* Stuttgart: Georg Thieme Verlag, (5th eds. Translated by M. W. Hamilton. Clinical Psychopathology. New York: Grune and Stratton, 1976.)

Shore, D., Andreasen, D. J. and Cutler, N. R. (1978). Prediction of self-mutilation in hospitalized schizophrenics. *American Journal of Psychiatry 135*:1406-1407.

Schweitzer I. 1990 Genital self-amputation and the Klingsor Syndrome. *Australian and New Zealand Journal of Psychiatry, 24*, 566-569.

Silva, J. A., Leong, G. B. and Weinstock, R. (1989). A case of skin and ear self-mutilation. *Psychosomatics, 30*, 228-230.

Silverstein, M. L. and Zerwic, M. J. (1985). Clinical psychopathologic symptoms in neuropsychologically impaired and intact schizophrenics. *Journal of Consulting and Clinical Psychology, 53*, 267-268.

Siris, S. G. (1991). Diagnosis of secondary depression in schizophrenia: Implications for DSM-IV. *Schizophrenia Bulletin, 17*, 75-98.

Snaith, P. (1992). Body image disorders. *Psychotherapy and Psychosomatics, 58*, 119-124.

Sonneburn, C. K. and Vanstraelen, P. M. (1992). A retsospective study on self-inflicted burns. *General Hospital Psychiatry, 14*, 404-407.

Spear, F. G. (1967). Pain in psychiatric patients. *Journal of Psychosomatic Research, 11*,187-193.

SPSS. (1997). *SPSS Base 7.5 Application Guide*. Chicago, Illinois: SPSS.

Spohn, H. E. and Strauss, M. E. (1989). Relation of neuroleptic and anticholinergic medication to cognitive functions in schizophrenia. *Journal of Abnormal Psychology, 98*, 367-380.

Strauss, M. E. (1993). Relations of symptoms to cognitive deficits in schizophrenia. *Schizophrenia Bulletin, 19*, 215-231.

Strauss, S. (1989). Subjective experiences of schizophrenia: Toward a new dynamic psychiatry – II. *Schizophrenia Bulletin, 15*, 179-187.

Sugarman, A. A. and Cancro, R. (1964). Field dependence and sophistication of body concept in schizophrenics. *Journal of Nervous and Mental Disease, 138*, 119-123.

Sweeny, S. and Zamecnik, K. (1981). Predictors of self-mutilation in patients with schizophrenia. *American Journal of Psychiatry, 138*, 1086-1089.

Swensen, C. H. (1957). Empirical evaluations of human figure drawings. *Psychological Bulletin, 54*, 431-466.

Swensen, C. H. (1968). Empirical evaluations of human figure drawings: 1957-1966. *Psychological Bulletin, 70*, 20-44.

Taylor, M. A. and Abrams, R. (1984). Cognitive dysfunction in schizophrenia. *American Journal of Psychiatry, 141*, 196-201.

Taylor, P. J. (1995). Schizophrenia and the risk of violence. In S. R. Hirsh and D. R. Weinberger (Eds). *Schizophrenia*. Oxford: Blackwell Science Ltd.

Tollefson, G. D., Sanger, T. M., Lu, Y. and Thieme, M.E. (1998). Depressive signs and symptoms in schizophrenia: a prospective blinded trial of olanzapine and haloperidol. *Archives of General Psychiatry, 55*, 250-258.

Torrey, E. F. (1989). Headache in schizophrenia and seasonality of births. *Biological Psychiatry, 26*, 847-858.

Traub, A. C., Olson, R., Orbach, J. and Cardone, S. C. (1967). Psychophysical studies of body image: III. Initial studies of disturbance in a chronic schizophrenic group. *Archives of General Psychiatry, 17*, 664-670.

Twemlow, S. W., Gabbard, G.O. and Jones, F. C. (1982). The out-of-body experience: a phenomenological typology based on questionnaire responses. *American Journal of Psychiatry, 139*, 450-455.

Urist, J. (1977). The Rorschach test and the assessment of object relations. *Journal of Personality Assessment, 41*, 3-9.

Vanderkampt, H. (1970). Clinical anomalies in patients with schizophrenia. *Experimental Medicine and Surgery, 28*, 291-293.

Van Puttan, T. and May, P. R. A. (1978). 'Akinetic depression' in schizophrenia. *Archives of General Psychiatry, 35*, 1101-1107.

Varsamis, J., Adamson, J. D. (1976). Somatic symptoms in schizophrenia. *Canadian Psychiatric Association Journal, 21*, 1-6.

Vincent, K. R. and Harman, M. J. (1991). The Exner Rorschach: an analysis of its clinical validity. *Journal of Clinical Psychology, 47*, 596-599.

Wagner, E. E. and Frye, D. (1990). Diagnostic and intellectual implications of the fragmented Rorschach W:D ratio. *Perceptual and Motor Skills, 71*, 887-890.

Watkins, J. and Stauffacher, J. (1952). An index of pathological thinking in the Rorschach. *Journal of Projective Techniques, 16*, 276-286.

Watson, G. D., Chandarana, P. C. and Merskey, H. (1981). Relationships between pain and schizophrenia. *British Journal of Psychiatry, 138*, 33-36.

Weckowicz, T. E. and Sommer, R. (1960). Body image and self-concept in schizophrenia, an experimental study. *Journal of Mental Science, 106*, 17-39.

Weinberger, D. R., Berman, K. F. and Zec, R. F. (1986). Physiologic dysfunction of dorsolateral prefrontal cortex in schizophrenia: I. Regional cerebral blood flow evidence. *Archives of General Psychiatry, 4*, 114-124.

Weinberger, D. R., Torrey, E. F., Neophytides, A. N. and Wyatt, R.J. (1979). Lateral cerebral ventricular enlargement in chronic schizophrenia. *Archives of General Psychiatry, 36*, 735-739.

Weiser, M., Levy, A. and Neuman, M. (1993). Ear Stuffing: An unusual form of self-mutilation. *Journal of Nervous and Mental Disease, 181*, 587-588.

West, B. M. and Hecker, A.O. (1952). Peptic ulcer: Incidence and diagnosis in psychotic patients. *American Journal of Psychiatry, 109*, 35-37.

Young, D. A., Davila, R. and Scher, H. (1993). Unawareness of illness and neuropsychological performance in chronic schizophrenia. *Schizophrenia Research, 10*, 117-124.

Zung, W. W. K. (1965). A self-rating depression scale. *Archives of General Psychiatry, 12*, 63-70.

INDEX

A

B

C

D

E

F

G

H

I

J

K

L

M

N

O

P

T

U

V

W

X